The Vagaries of

L. Allen Harker

Alpha Editions

This edition published in 2024

ISBN : 9789362098054

Design and Setting By
Alpha Editions
www.alphaedis.com
Email - info@alphaedis.com

Contents

FOREWORD

A small boy coming down to the drawing-room at half-past five for the sacred hour of play, found a visitor absorbing his mother's attention. For five minutes or so he politely refrained from interrupting their conversation, and he wandered about the room, a little disconsolate perhaps, but in that state of being described by nurses as "not a bit of trouble." When, however, the five minutes lengthened into ten, he felt that direct action of some sort was imperative. So he advanced upon the lingering guest, laid small, imperative hands upon her knee; and lifting an anxious face to hers, enquired in honeyed tones: "Is you going to stay very much longer?"

That was in the forgotten, by some regretted, by many derided, nineties.

The other day I was having tea with a charming friend, wise mother of many sons, when the youngest, aged two, came for the sacred hour. It was pleasant in that drawing-room and I made no haste to go. Whereupon he came to me and, with a gracious, even a gallant, gesture, held out his hand to me with the utmost friendliness, conversing the while perpetually and emphatically in a manner difficult for the uninitiated to follow. Pleased and flattered, I took the kind little hand, which pulled me to my feet. He then firmly led me to the door and out to the top of the staircase, and was preparing to escort me downstairs and to the front door, when his mother ran after us and fetched us back.

[viii]Whatever else is changing in the present; bewildering world, there is one section of the community that is essentially Conservative, not to say "Die Hard."

Outside my window there is a long, straggling street of old cottages which have altered very little since the fourteenth century, and in those little old houses dwell many children who play in the street, games that were doubtless popular "in Thebes's streets three thousand years ago."

The adult attitude towards children has changed even during the last fifty years, and largely for the better. Yet the child's attitude towards his playmate, and even towards the omniscient grown-up, is fundamentally what it has been throughout the ages.

The early nineteenth century is often quoted by deprecators of the twentieth as a time when the attitude of youth towards age was particularly praiseworthy in its modesty and reverence. Such people, who are perhaps a little prone to forget their own youthful viewpoint, tell us that in those golden days children accepted without question the opinions of those who were set in authority over them, and were almost invariably obedient, contented and unenterprising. Yet, researches in the literature published especially for children by that "friend of youth," John Newbery, at "the corner of St. Paul's Churchyard," in his little "gilt books"—most of them published between 1745 and 1802—prove that badly-behaved children were by no means uncommon, and that over-indulgent parents were not unknown. In the "Histories of More Children than One; or, Goodness Better than[ix] Beauty," Master John and Miss Mary Strictum, who, as their names imply, are models of deportment, are unfavorably contrasted with Master Thomas and Miss Kitty Bloomer.

Thomas insists upon his papa's horse being brought into the parlour for him to ride round the room. His mamma tried "to persuade him not to want it, but he would have his own way."

"Thomas was much pleased to have it, but Kitty was afraid of it and did not like that it should stay. She therefore began to scream and beg it might go out. 'Pray take it out!' said she. 'It shall go out; it shan't stay.'

"'It shan't go out. It shall stay!' said her brother.

"They made such a noise that they frightened the horse, and he began to kick and prance," and all manner of disasters followed. Not even the most weak-minded modern parent could go further than this in the way of indulgence.

Even in so didactic a work as "The First Principles of Religion and the *Existence of a Deity Explained in a Series of Dialogues Adapted to the Capacity of the Infant Mind,*" you will find a child as human and engaging as any infant born since the Armistice. In this work the particular infant selected for enlightenment is one Maria, made after no formal pattern. Throughout the long and deadly dialogues her nimble mind outpaces mamma's ponderous aphorisms. As, when that lady discourses on the awful consequences of taking God's name in vain, Maria demands demurely: "But would it not be politer and prettier to say either Mr. or Mrs., and not plain God?"

[x]Again, when her mother, as an example of the evils of slyness, relates how "the two Misses Quick had pincushions of the same make, but Miss Betty's was larger than Miss Sally's," and Miss Sally by a subterfuge manages to exchange her own for her sister's, Maria says thoughtfully: "Do you think then, Mamma, that it signifies to God which of the Miss Quicks had the larger pincushion?"

Could the most recent Realist ask a more searching question?

At Christmas time the papers seemed full of descriptions of *blasé* children who insisted on going to expensive shops to choose their own presents, who scoffed at fairies or Santa Claus, and scouted the idea of any sort of childlike party. I do not move in plutocratic circles, so I cannot vouch for either the truth or falsehood of these dismal revelations. But I do know that the vast majority of gently-bred children born before and during the years that followed 1914 are easily pleased, and are grateful for very small mercies in the way of amusement, because nothing else is possible to the greater part of the upper middle class for financial reasons. And no one who, in recent years, has been to "Peter Pan" and looked round the crowded theatre gloriously garlanded with chubby, rosy faces, and heard the full-throated affirmative that greets the question "Do you believe in fairies?" can doubt that children are still pretty sound on subjects of that sort.

This being so, is it incredibly bold or superlatively simple, on my part, to have ventured to collect into a little sheaf some fugitive sketches of the kind of children I have known during the last twenty-five years?

[xi]Perhaps it is, and that being so, I can only quote the lines in which Mr. Kipling has once and for all time summed up the humble plea of the free-lance:

When 'Omer smote 'is bloomin' lyre,

He'd 'eard men sing by land an' sea;

An' what he thought 'e might require,

'E went an' took—the same as me!

CIRENCESTER
1923

- 3 -

PART I
BOYS

I
THE MURDER

By the people who live in the same terrace they are known as "those dreadful twins." By the more plain-spoken of the masters at the preparatory school which they attend they are distinguished by an adjective whose meaning is the reverse of "heavenly"; and their schoolfellows are filled with respectful admiration for the boys, the most resourcefully and superfluously naughty of their acquaintance, whose genius for making the most patient of masters lose his temper is unsurpassed.

The only person who takes them and their ways with calm philosophy is their mother. She, with that sense of proportion and balanced wisdom so frequently vouchsafed to mothers of large families, laughs and loves them, and believes in their ultimate regeneration. There is some ground for the faith that is in her; for when a woman has seen six sons fare forth into the world to cut no such indifferent figure in it, she is not apt to despair of the two youngest, roister they never so.

[2]Moreover, she declares that most of their evil doings are "really Mr. Stevenson's fault," and there is truth in the charge, for from the moment that some thoughtless person, probably a godfather (I have known godfathers, living at a distance, who would present trumpets, nay, even concertinas! to the sons of men whom they have called by the name of friend), gave Peter a copy of "The Merry Men" and Tod "Treasure Island," they have tried to fit their surroundings to the characters they are forever enacting; with the result that the plain workaday world, that knows not the "Master Mage" of Samoa, is always puzzled and generally wroth.

That genial "spirit of boyhood" had never so much as to beckon to them; he had but to hold out his friendly hands, and Tod and Peter, each clasping one in both their own, were his, body and soul, forevermore.

They are alike as the two Dromios, these twins; and the mistakes and complications arising from this likeness are a never-failing source of satisfaction to them. For instance, Peter will cheerfully undergo a caning intended for Tod that he may afterwards meekly demand of his chastener what he has done to deserve this discipline, gleefully watching the while the weary wonder on the master's face grow to a disgusted certainty that he has, as usual, "punished the wrong one."

The fact that they are rather noticeably comely boys—they came of a family where on both sides of the house good looks are the invariable rule—only serves to increase the confusion. Both aretall and straight, fair-haired, blue-eyed, ruddy, and of a uniformly cheerful countenance. But kind Nature has bestowed on Tod an accomplishment she has denied to Peter, to his lasting grief.

At certain seasons of the year Tod "moults" and can pull out quantities of his thick fair hair without the slightest inconvenience to himself. He generally chooses to perform this feat during the silent hours of "prep." They have done their evening work at school ever since the night they were discovered grilling "Home Influence" and "A Mother's Recompense" over the study fire, when they ought to have been wrestling with "Excerpta Facilia." When the master in charge has walked down to the end of the long schoolroom where Tod "keeps," and has turned to go back again, Tod is suddenly seized by a perfect paroxysm of despair, clutches at his hair with frantic though absolute noiseless gesticulations, and casts whole handfuls of fluffy curls on the floor about him.

Naturally his companions, including Peter, get lines for disturbing the placidity of "prep" with their unseemly giggles. And George, when he sweeps up the schoolroom next morning, may be heard to mutter:

"Wherever all this 'air do come from passes me!"

Tod's real name is Percy—he is called after a wealthy and aristocratic relative—but he refuses point-blank to answer to it, for he fancies that it savours of those "eeny peeny" children in "Home Influence," a work that earned their undying hatredwhen it was read aloud to them by a well-intentioned but mistaken aunt while they were recovering from measles.

On the occasion of its holocaust, before referred to, their mother, passing the study, and struck by the unwonted stillness reigning therein, opened the door softly and looked in. Both boys were stooping over the fireplace and prodding a solid yet feathery mass that glowed and gloomed in the heart of the embers.

"There goes Herbert, 'the almost-angel boy,' and 'haughty Caroline,' and 'playful Emmiline,'" whispered Tod, poking viciously. While Peter, quoting from "Thrawn Janet," added in an awful voice:

"Witch, beldame, devil! I charge you, by the power of God, begone—if you be dead, to the grave—if you be damned, to hell."

I regret to say that their mother's sense of humor is stronger than her dislike of strong language, and that she stole away to laugh, leaving the conspirators unrebuked for the moment. But they did their "prep." at school henceforth.

Peter's manner is singularly misleading in its frank sincerity, and he will on occasion answer a sudden question in a way which is, to say the least of it, bewildering to his interlocutor.

For instance, one day in the football-field a new master asked him the name of a small boy some distance off who was "slacking" abominably.

"Who's that chap with the red hair by the goal posts?" he said to Peter, who had been somewhat officiously putting him right on several points.

[5]"Dumpkins, sir," that youth replied, demurely, and strolled off to a distant part of the playground.

"Dumpkins!" bawled the master. "Dumpkins, why aren't you playing up?"

But Dumpkins heeded not the voice of authority and continued to loll and gaze heavenward in easy inactivity.

"Dumpkins! Dump-kins!" again he bellowed.

But Dumpkins only took an apple out of his pocket and began to eat it.

He is a hasty-tempered young man that master, and he strode toward the hapless Dumpkins and shook him angrily, exclaiming:

"Why don't you answer when I call, you cheeky little beggar?"

"Please, sir, you never called me, sir," expostulated the boy, wriggling in the master's grip.

"Why, I've been shouting 'Dumpkins' all over the field for the last five minutes!"

"But, please sir, my name is Jones!"

"Why did you tell me Jones's name was Dumpkins, you, Peter?" the master indignantly demanded of Tod some minutes later.

"I couldn't have done that, sir," said Tod, gravely, "for there's nobody called Dumpkins in the school."

It was this young master who rechristened the twins when Peter next day insisted that "a point has position but no gratitude."

Strangely enough "The Merry Men" finds even greater favor with them than "Treasure Island," and with the enigmatical decision of childhoodtheir favorite of all the stories is "Markheim," not "Will o' the Mill," beloved of critics. It is doubtful if they understand much of it, but nevertheless they read it over and over again to each other aloud, or silently with their curly heads pressed together, till they knew it by heart. To be sure, "Thrawn Janet" has a dreadful fascination for them, and they acted one of the principal scenes with somewhat direful results.

Peter made Tod "tie him by the neck" to the bed with red worsted, while Tod, in his character of the minister, had to creep in, candle in hand, to discover the dread spectacle; and Peter's representation of the fearsome Janet was so truthful and blood-curdling that Tod dropped the candle and fled downstairs howling at the top of his voice, and such was his haste that he fell and sprained his wrist. Meanwhile, the candle had set fire to the valance of the bed, and altogether there was a fine hullabaloo; there was also an end put to their dramatic efforts for a week or two.

Nothing daunted, however, about a month later, on a Sunday evening when the servants were all at church, and their mother writing for dear life the long weekly letters that have to be written when a woman has husband and four sons scattered about the globe, Tod and Peter sought the seclusion of the kitchen and determined to "act" "Markheim."

All went well and quietly for a long time; the firelit kitchen with loud ticking clock answered admirably as the scene of the murder, the dialogue between Markheim and the mysterious strangerwent without a hitch, and Tod sallied forth into a "wonderful clear night of stars," while Peter shut the back door softly after him. Peter, in his character of Markheim, was bent upon making the speech with which the story concludes, where the maidservant rings the door-bell and Markheim opens to her with the words: "You had better go for the police; I have killed your master!"

Poor Tod had to be the maidservant—he always had to follow where Peter led. He shivered as he ran up the area steps; it was a cold night, he had not troubled to provide himself with a coat, and his heart was heavy, for, to tell the truth, he has far more imagination than Peter, and sometimes their plays are to him one long agony of apprehension.

He positively dreaded ringing that area bell, and the sinister announcement that would follow on the act. No longer was he Tod, but a trembling servant lass who was forced by fate to ring a bell which sounded a tocsin of dreadful import.

He ran down to the end of the terrace and stood under a lamp that he might brace himself for the final effort.

Meanwhile, Peter, swollen with importance at the thought of the mighty sensation he would make in a minute or two, stood squeezed against the hinge of the door waiting for the fateful ring.

Then came a patter of light feet down the area steps and someone gave the bell a modest pull. Peter drew open the door with great suddenness upon himself, exclaiming in a deep and tragic voice, the result of long practice in solitary attics:

[8]*"You had better go for the police; I have killed your master!"*

The visitor gave a piercing shriek and rushed up the steps again, calling breathlessly upon Heaven and the police. Peter, behind the door, wagged his head, exclaiming admiratively:

"How well that kid does act; I could almost declare I heard skirts rustling."

Peter waited awhile for his brother to return and be congratulated, but Tod didn't appear, so he concluded that he had gone round to the front door and come in that way; besides, the servants were just due from church, and cook would be cross if she found him in her domain. He ran upstairs and waited for his twin in the drawing-room. His mother looked up from her letters and smiled at the little figure tip-toeing on the hearth-rug to admire himself in the glass. Then scratch, scratch went her pen again.

Now, Ada, the housemaid, has a dear friend in service at the other end of the terrace, and she attends a church where the sermons are shorter than those at the one frequented by Peter's household. On this particular Sunday she got out of church quite early and thought she would see whether Ada happened to be in. Thus, while Tod with lagging feet crept slowly down the terrace from one end, she was already fleeing affrightedly to the other in search of the nearest policeman.

She found him at the pillar-box, and fell into his stalwart arms, crying hysterically:

"Oh, come quick! There's bin murder done at Number 9. Someone's bin an' killed the marster!"

[9]P.C. Lee turned the light of his bull's-eye upon Ada's friend and found her fair to look upon. All the same, although he still supported her trembling frame, he shook his head slowly, saying:

"'E ain't there for to be murdered; the Colonel's bin in Hinjia this las' ten weeks; the missis tol' me so 'erself, when she ast me to keep a special heye to them premises."

All the same, in spite of his incredulity, P.C. Lee was already on his way to Number 9, half leading, half carrying Ada's friend with him.

"But I tell you," persisted the girl, "when I ring that there bell, the door opened sudden-like as if someone was be'ind it, and a hawful voice says to me, 'You'd better go for the perlice,' it says, 'I've killed your master,' and I was that taken to, I did go for you, Mr. Lee, as fast as I could lay foot to the ground. It may be as one of the young gentlemen's bin murdered, 'is pa bein', so to speak, abroad. It give me such a turn——"

And Ada's friend was forced to stop in the middle of the road, overcome by the horrid recollection.

"But didn't you see no one?" asked P.C. Lee, in a judicial voice.

"No, trust me, I didn't wait to *see* nothing; I'd 'eard enough without that. I'll wait out 'ere," she continued as they reached the scene of the tragedy, "on the top of the steps. I couldn't abear to see no dead bodies;" and Ada's friend disengaged herself from the policeman's protecting clasp and clung to the area railings for support, exclaiming afresh: "I'd never get over it—never!"

"But you must come in and give evidence wot you did 'ear," expostulated P.C. Lee. "I don't believe myself as anything criminal 'as occurred; but I'll just ring and ast."

"I'd take my dyin' oath them was the very words that murderer says to me," cried Ada's friend, jibbing on the top step as the minion of the law put forth a large hand to assist her down. "'I've killed your master,' says 'e, despairin' like, as if it was no use to try an' 'ide it."

P.C. Lee proceeded to perform a solo on the bell very different to the two timid tintinnabulations that had preceded it during the last ten minutes; for while Ada's friend sought the protection of the strong arm of the law, poor little Tod had screwed his courage to the sticking-point, gone back and rung the area bell, when, to his unspeakable relief, he was admitted by cook, just returned from church in so benign a humor that she forebore to scold him for being out at such untoward hours "without so much as a 'at," and bestowed a piece of bread and dripping upon him "to stop 'is teeth a-chatterin'."

Whereupon, comforted and refreshed, he departed to find Peter.

Meanwhile P.C. Lee insisted that he must see the missis, for Ada's friend was unshaken in her evidence, question they never so, and the four maids at Number 9 declared that they could not sleep comfortably in their beds unless the search-light of his bull's-eye was thrown on every dusky corner of the house by P.C. Lee himself before he took his departure.

Ada's friend was seated weeping in the front hall surrounded by the others, when the mistress, fetched by Ada herself, and accompanied by Tod and Peter, descended to hold parley with P.C. Lee.

"I can't understand it, ma'am," concluded the policeman, after a long explanation, continually interrupted by Ada's friend with such interpolations as: "Oh, a hawful voice, that mournful"—"Them was the very words," etc.

During this recital Tod and Peter crept further and further into the background, nudging each other in the ecstasy occasioned by such an unexpected tribute to their histrionic powers.

But their mother knows her Stevenson—and the twins—so before the narrative was nearly finished she turned swiftly upon them, demanding sternly:

"Which of you was it?"

"Young varmints!" said P.C. Lee to Ada's friend, as he escorted her home; "I might 'a' knowed it was them. 'Tain't the fust time I've come across 'em, neither...."

II
THE SENDING

When the time came for those twins, Tod and Peter, to go to public school, their mother seriously considered the advisability of putting them into different "houses." At first she thought that, perhaps, it might make for righteousness to separate them. But on hearing the subject mooted, they so whole-heartedly fell in with her opinion, rapturously reviewing the possibility of "changing houses" whenever they felt so inclined, that she instantly dismissed the idea; rightly coming to the conclusion that if their extraordinary resemblance was a cause of general muddle and mystification while they were together, it would become confusion worse confounded were they separated. Moreover, she reflected that even schoolmasters are men of like passions with ourselves, and rightly refrained from adding to such a one's already heavy burden by a separate superintendence of the twins.

Tod and Peter, whose mental attitude was always that "all is for the best in the best possible of worlds," decided that after all propinquity has its advantages, and rejoiced that family tradition sent them into a house whose head was proverbially the "slackest old slackster in the whole school." A dreamy, mild-mannered, gentlemanly man that master, who left the management of the "house" entirely to an extremely energetic wife and a "young brusher" ("brusher" is the familiar term for master in that school), whose prowess in the playing-fields was only equalled by his extreme fussiness where rules of his own making were concerned.

"Not a bad chap," the twins decided after their first week; "but a bit like the German Emperor, you know—wants things all his own way. Still, if you humor the youth, he's all right."

So successfully did they humor the "young brusher" in question that for the first month all went smoothly, and the house-master himself, a gentle optimist, ever ready to believe the best of boy-humanity, really thought that the "character" that had preceded them from preparatory school was perhaps over-emphasized.

Their late headmaster, while giving them full credit for general integrity and fair abilities, had, in mercy to his brethren of the craft, pointed out that they were ever "ready to join in frivolity and insubordination, when not under my own eye." They had to work, for they were on the Modern Side, and destined for the army, and in that particular school, not the wiliest shirker in creation can escape the argus eye of the "head of the Modern," or the retribution, swift, sharp, and sure, that follows any such line of conduct.

But, bless you! ordinary work and games, at which both were good, never found sufficient scope for the energies of Tod and Peter, and by the time the first month was up they began their tricks.

One Mr. Neatby, M.A., taught the twins chemistry. Not that they went to him together. They were in different, though, as far as work went, parallel forms, and finding that their systematic "changing" was never so much as suspected, and therefore carried with it no spice of danger or adventure, they gave it up, devoting their energies to the tormenting of Mr. Neatby, who had by his severity incurred their august displeasure.

Mr. Neatby was tall, severe, and dignified. He really liked his subject, but felt, as a rule, little affection for his pupils. Nevertheless, he was conscientious to the last degree in the discharge of his duties. His way of expressing himself was what Peter called "essayish"; he gave lines lavishly, and had but little mercy on the reckless breaker of test-tubes. He did not rant, or stamp, or call people by opprobrious names, as did many better loved masters. He was always cold, cutting, and superior. But the thing about him that most excited Peter's animosity was his necktie.

"He wears revolting, jerry-built, Judas-like ties," the indignant Peter proclaimed to an admiring audience of lower boys; "ties that slip down and show a beastly, brassy stud. His socks, too, leave much to be desired; in fact, his extremities altogether are such as betoken a bad, hard heart."

"Let me see," said Tod softly, looking up from a book he was reading; "do you think that a *sending* might soften the man's hard heart?"

At this particular stage of the twins' career, Mr. Kipling was the God of their idolatry, and both of them had "gloated," even in the manner of the immortal "Stalky" himself, over the vengeance of Ram Das.

"It might be managed," Peter answered, thoughtfully scratching his smooth chin; "but then again, it may be close-time for kittens just at present; don't they generally bloom in the spring?"

"There's always plenty of kittens, you juggins," ejaculated a prosaic friend. "Why, when I was down at the riding school this morning, there was a cat with six in an empty loose-box; they'll have to drown five of 'em, they told me. D'your people want one or what?"

"*I* want one," Peter rejoined excitedly; "not one, but five, to give to a dear friend."

"Shouldn't think he'd be your dear friend long."

"Oh, yes, he will. He's an S.P.C.K., or whatever it is. He's awfully profane—humane, I mean."

"Well," said the other boy, still unconvinced; "you can ask about 'em when you go for your lesson to-morrow morning. They weren't half bad little beasts, but I shouldn't advise you to give your friend more than one at a time, anyhow."

Both Tod and Peter went twice a week to the riding school in the town, as they were both destined for cavalry. Every underling about the place knew them well, and liked them. Their father had lived in the town during his last leave, jobbed his horses at the riding-master's stables, and had himself assisted at the lessons of elder brothers of Tod and Peter.

Now there was at the school a certain Figgins, a generally handy man, or rather boy, who worshipped the ground the twins walked upon; and after their next lesson they and Figgins might have been seen holding long and earnest parley in the loose-box containing the cat and kittens.

The twins laughed uproariously all the way home, and just as they reached the house, Peter remarked: "I hate anything dead. Figgins has promised not one of 'em shall be drowned, and when they're fit to be moved, he'll tell old White he's found good homes for the lot. And then—and then Tod, my boy! our dear teacher shall have 'em alive, 'alive, all alive oh! alive, all alive oh!'" and Peter burst into song in the exuberance of his joy.

Mr. Neatby lived in lodgings within a convenient distance of the school. He was therefore spared any intercourse with the boys after school hours, and usually spent his evenings in correcting innumerable marble-boarded exercise books, containing chemistry notes. He was so engaged one evening about nine o'clock, when his landlady entered the room and laid a square parcel at his elbow.

He finished correcting the book he had in hand, and took another, when his attention was arrested by an indescribable sound.

Mr. Neatby lifted his head and gazed about the room. "Could it be a mouse under the skirting-board?" he wondered. Then half unconsciously his eyes fell on the parcel his landlady had brought into the room. It was an oblong cardboard box, about the size of an ordinary shoe-box. But, although tied up with string, it was not wrapped in paper, and on looking at it more closely, Mr. Neatby discovered that the top was riddled with small holes.

Had it been summer, he, being something of a naturalist, would have at once concluded that someone had sent him some rare caterpillars, but what caterpillars are to be found in November?

He drew the parcel toward him, and there arose that curious sound again, louder and more insistent. He hastily cut the string and removed the lid of the box, and inside, reposing on a nest of hay, lay a very young and mewey kitten. A kitten who most evidently was homesick and aggrieved at being reft from the maternal bosom. A sprawly, squirmy, noisy kitten, that immediately proceeded to climb out of the box and crawl uncertainly to Mr. Neatby's blotting-pad, where it collapsed into a dismal little heap, mewing louder than ever.

"There must be some mistake," muttered Mr. Neatby, flushed and perturbed. "No one would send *me* a kitten; that stupid woman must have made some muddle or other," and he arose hastily and rang the bell.

He so rarely rang his bell after his modest supper had been cleared away that Mrs. Vyner, his landlady, had given up expecting him to do so, and had on this occasion "just stepped out," as she would have put it, to see a neighbor.

Mr. Neatby rang, and rang in vain, finally so far departing from his decorously distant demeanor as to go to the top of the kitchen stairs and shout. But the faint mewing of the kitten was the only answer to his outcries, and baffled and annoyed he returned to his sitting-room to find that the kitten had upset the red ink over Tod's chemistry notes, which, in company with many others, lay open on the table, and was feebly attempting to lap it up.

"Poor little thing; it's hungry," he thought to himself. And being, indeed, as Peter said, a very humane man, he lifted it from the table, and went to his sideboard to see if he could find any milk. He did find some in the cupboard underneath where it had no business to be, and pouring some into a saucer, laid it on the floor beside the kitten, who proceeded to refresh itself with commendable promptitude.

Then, as his landlady still made no appearance, Mr. Neatby bethought him of looking at the parcel to see whether the kitten had been left at the wrong house. But no; attached to the string was a label, clearly addressed in a flowing, clerkly hand, "S. S. Neatby, Esq., M.A.," followed by his address, accurate as to number, street, and even town.

Once more he sat down in his chair, and leant his head on his hand to think, when he perceived, tucked into the hay at one side of the box, a card, and drew it forth hastily; a plain glazed visiting card on which was inscribed the words, "From a grateful friend," in the same excellent handwriting as the label.

Mr. Neatby blushed, and looked guiltily at the happily supping kitten. In addition to being humane, Mr. Neatby was also charitable, and there were many poor who had reason to be grateful to him. But as he always gave alms through a third person, and was one of those modest people who take care that their left hand knows not what the right hand doeth, he felt quite upset.

Presently he heard his landlady and her niece come in, and rang again.

"Who brought this box, Mrs. Vyner?" he asked, holding it up toward her.

"I can't say, sir, I'm sure. It was dark when I answered the door, and a young man—leastways, I think 'e was young—simply give it into my 'ands and ran down the steps again. I 'eld it under the gas in the 'all, sir, and read the label, as it was for you right enough, so I brings it in and lays it down without never interruptin' you, sir, like you said."

"*There was a kitten in that box,*" Mr. Neatby said solemnly, in such a tone as might have announced some national calamity.

"Sakes alive! you don't say so, sir," cried Mrs. Vyner in great excitement; "shall you keep it, sir?"

"I don't know yet," Mr. Neatby said gravely; "it must stay here for to-night anyway."

"It's a pretty little thing, sir," said the landlady, stooping down to look at it where it lay basking in the heat of the fire. "'Twould be company for you, wouldn't it, sir?"

"Hadn't it better go with you to the kitchen for to-night, Mrs. Vyner?" Mr. Neatby asked persuasively, and Mrs. Vyner, with many protestations of wonder, gathered up the kitten into her apron and departed to the lower regions, where she informed the niece who lived with her that their lodger "'adn't spoken so many words to 'er never before, no, not in a month of Sundays."

Mr. Neatby threw the box into his capacious waste-paper basket, but he put the card and label carefully away in one of the pigeon-holes of his desk.

Next day, on his return from morning school, he found a white cardboard hat-box, big enough to contain the most umbrageous matinée hat ever worn, set right in the middle of his table, and he felt distinctly annoyed. His landlady followed him into the sitting-room to lay lunch, and he, pointing to the offending box, said coldly: "I must ask you not to leave your parcels in my room, Mrs. Vyner."

Mrs. Vyner bridled, and seizing the box, held it out toward him, remarking aggrievedly: "If so be as you refers to this 'ere, sir, I must ast you to look 'oo it's addressed to. It's put plain enough for you, sir."

"But I assure you," Mr. Neatby cried, recoiling from the proffered hat-box, "that I haven't ordered a hat of any kind."

"Any'ow," said Mrs. Vyner scornfully, "I don't suppose, sir, as you'd order your 'ats from Madame Looeese, if you 'ad. I thought per'aps you'd bought a present for your young lady."

"Mrs. Vyner," replied Mr. Neatby, in a voice glacial as liquid air itself, "you forget yourself."

Mrs. Vyner set down the box with an angry thump, and proceeded to lay the cloth in injured silence.

When she had gone, Mr. Neatby approached the mysterious package delicately, much as though it had been an infernal machine of some sort, and regarded it searchingly on all sides. It most certainly emanated from the millinery establishment of "Madame Louise," but was none the less certainly addressed in sprawly, feminine handwriting to "S. S. Neatby, Esq., M.A."

Just then Mrs. Vyner opened the door, saying waspishly, "'Ere's your kitting, sir; it keeps getting under my feet while I'm dishin' up."

It seemed to have gained considerable vigor during the night, for it rushed across the room and up the curtain.

But Mr. Neatby had screwed his courage to the sticking-place, and even the tempestuous entry of the kitten could not turn him from his purpose. Penknife in hand, he cut the string of the bonnet-box, and lifted the lid timidly, prepared no doubt for some tissue-paper protected "confection" within. When, lo! even as that of the shoe-box on the previous night was this interior; hay, dry and fragrant of stable, met his astonished gaze, while seated in its midst was a tabby kitten, who gathered herself together for a spring the instant the lid was lifted, and sprang with such good-will as to turn the box over on its side, when she immediately dashed under the table.

Mr. Neatby gazed, as if hypnotized, at the tumbled box, till the rattling of dishes outside warned him of the near approach of his landlady with lunch, and roused him from his trance.

He stooped hastily, thrust the scattered hay into the band-box, clapped on the lid, and placed it under the knee-hole of his writing-table.

The door was opened rather suddenly to admit Mrs. Vyner; kitten number one descended from the curtain, and Mr. Neatby found himself almost praying that kitten number two would stay under the table while his landlady was in the room. Mrs. Vyner glanced disdainfully in the direction of the band-box, noted that the string had been cut, set the dishes on the table with somewhat unnecessary violence, and departed without having opened her lips, just as the two kittens frisked out from beneath the table.

Mr. Neatby, harrassed and flushed "all over his eminent forehead," did not begin his lunch. He went back to the band-box again, studied the label anew, and finally rummaged in the hay inside.

His search was rewarded by the discovery of a rather dirty piece of paper, on which was written "A Present from Framilode," Framilode being a village in the neighborhood, celebrated for the manufacture of a certain kind of mug which always bore that legend. He put it carefully beside the other card and label in his desk, and returned to his lunch with but small appetite, and a frown of perplexity upon his brow. The kittens set up a perfect chorus of mewing; Mr. Neatby braced himself to explain the new arrival to Mrs. Vyner, and rang for the pudding.

"It's my belief, sir," said Mrs. Vyner that evening, "that somebody's a puttin' a 'oaf upon you. I sent my niece to that there Madame Looeese's with the box lid, an' she see madame 'erself, and *she* says as it's a hold box, an' that they certainly never sent you no box, nor wouldn't think of such a liberty, and you one of the school gentlemen and all. But my niece, she said as madame did laugh when she 'eard about the kitten, and 'er young ladies, too."

Mr. Neatby writhed.

To a man of his reserved and sensitive temperament, the reflection that his name could by any possibility be bandied about by a milliner and her assistants was little short of maddening. If he could then and there have ordered Mrs. Vyner "to take five hundred lines," it might have given him some relief. But in all things he was a just man, and he knew that his landlady had at all events meant kindly in trying to discover the perpetrator of the outrage; for the fact remained that somebody had most assuredly "put a 'oax" on him in the shape of the liveliest of tabby kittens.

It never occurred to him to suspect any of the boys. For how could one of them come by either band-box or kittens? To be sure there were some day boys, but it happened that these were nearly all "on the Classical," and Mr. Neatby had but little to do with them.

Of course he reckoned without the ubiquitous Figgins, who, unlike Mr. Neatby, *had* a young lady, who was employed by Madame Louise, and for whom it was an easy matter both to procure a disused band-box and a new label.

"You're certain he got them all right?" whispered Peter to Figgins at his next lesson, as that worthy rushed forward officiously to settle the sack on the horse's back. "He gave me back my notes simply smothered in red ink, and I thought I saw a mark like a kitten's paw, but I couldn't be sure."

"Law bless you! yes, sir, 'e got 'em right enough. I took 'em myself, and wot's more, both of 'em's there still, for I passed by this mornin' and 'appened to look down the airey, and there they both was as peart as print. I s'pose we'd better wait a day or so for the next 'un, 'adn't us?"

"Yes, Figgins, wait two days till you see me again," and Peter dug his knees into his horse and rode at the first jump.

"It's rather decent of him to *keep* them," thought Peter to himself, who was tender-hearted where animals were concerned. "Perhaps, if he doesn't clap on any more lines for a bit, I'll let him off with two."

But, alas for good intentions. When Peter got back to the house, he found Tod bursting with indignation. For at "Practical Chemistry," that very morning, Tod, who was supposed to be engaged in the manufacture of hydrogen, used so many conflicting ingredients as to cause an explosion and dense smoke, and a smell so appalling that it drove the whole class into the corridor, and caused several testy masters to send indignant messages demanding where the infernal smell came from.

Mr. Neatby, exasperated to the last degree, not only told Tod to take five hundred lines, but bade him return the very next half-holiday and spend the afternoon in doing similar experiments under his master's supervision.

Tod confided his grievance to Peter at great length, and concluded his recital with the injunction, "Let him have all three, the *beast*! I wish they were young gorillas."

Mr. Neatby was very busy. He was taking extra duty for a master who was ill, and for three or four days after the arrival of the second kitten really had not a moment to call his own, so, as Mrs. Vyner seemed to take quite kindly to the new arrivals—only taking care to charge her lodger an extra quart of milk daily for their maintenance—he almost forgot their existence.

By Saturday evening he had accumulated a mass of mid-term examination work to correct, and directly after supper set himself down to it, with four clear hours before him, for he often worked till after midnight.

His lamp was trimmed, his fire burned brightly, and one kitten, the first, sat purring on the hearth. That, and the scratching of Mr. Neatby's pen as he corrected the generally mistaken views of boys as to the nature of an element, were the only sounds till there came a thunderous rap outside, and the door-bell pealed loudly.

Mr. Neatby frowned, but never looked up from his corrections. He had not been long at the school, and was not upon intimate terms with any of the masters, so that it was hardly likely to be a caller for him. He heard somebody open the front door, then some vehicle drive away. A moment later there was a knock at his door, and Jemima, Mrs. Vyner's niece, came in, bearing a hamper.

"Please, sir, this 'ave just come by rail; there wasn't nothing to pay."

"Very well," Mr. Neatby answered without looking up; "put it down, please; I can't attend to it just now."

Jemima did as she was told, and once more silence settled upon the room.

But not for long. Kitten number one got restless; it walked round and round the hamper, and sniffed and mewed, and mewed and sniffed, with irritating persistency. Moreover, a curious muffled echo seemed to accompany its mewing. Mr. Neatby bore it for five minutes, then pushed back his chair, caught the disturbing kitten by the scruff of its neck, and bore it to the top of the kitchen stairs, calling to Jemima to take it down. That young lady obeyed his summons, taking the kitten tenderly into her arms with many endearments; but all the same she remarked to her aunt, "Well, I do think as 'e might manage to look after *one* on 'em 'isself, that I do."

Mr. Neatby went back to his papers and corrected with more vigor than before; but, in spite of his haste, in spite of his absorption, the muffled mewing continued.

At last he laid down his pen and listened. "Surely," he thought, "it can't sound like that from downstairs. I must have got the sound on my nerves; it's really most annoying." It *was* annoying; it grew louder and louder till it seemed at his very side.

Mr. Neatby was endowed with great powers, both of self-control and concentration. Having decided that the sound was in his imagination, and not actual, he went on with the paper that he was correcting, but as he placed it on the top of the growing pile he chanced to notice the hamper which was placed on the hearth-rug close beside him. "Apples, I suppose, from home," he thought to himself; "but all the same, I'd better see." He lifted it on to his knee. "Too light for apples," he thought again. "What can they have sent?"

The lid was not very tightly fastened, and a slash or two of the penknife at the string restraining it brought it away.

Hay, and again hay, in this case forming the cosy nest of *two* kittens, one tortoiseshell and one black. Both lively and vociferous beyond either of their predecessors. Mr. Neatby ejaculated just one word, and sat perfectly still with the open hamper on his knee. The kittens climbed out and made hay among his papers, but he took no notice. "An angry man was he," and when a man of his temperament is angry, he usually sits tight. The kittens got tired of the table, and jumped lightly to the floor, carrying a few dozen papers with them in their flight, but still Mr. Neatby sat on staring into space.

When at last he roused himself, he once more sought some solution of the mystery in the address label, but the yellow railway label on the back had been torn away, and only "ton" remained. The address itself was printed very neatly by hand.

Inside the hamper he found a little pink envelope with nicked edges such as servants love. He opened it, and printed by the same hand, on a piece of paper to match, was the following verse:

The kitten's a persistent beast,

It comes when you expect it least,

It comes in ones, it comes in twos—

And when it comes it always mews.

"Ah!" Mr. Neatby said softly to himself, "some boy is at the bottom of this."

The clock struck twelve, and he remembered with a start that both his landlady and Jemima would certainly be in bed.

What was to be done with the kittens?

He was far too kind-hearted to turn them out of doors on a cold November night. They were really uncommonly pretty little beasts, and as he watched their gambles he found himself quoting:

Alas! regardless of their doom,

The little victims play,

and then realized that they had no business to be playing at all at that time of night, and that he certainly wanted to go to bed.

He really was a much tried man that night. First, he had to catch the kittens and put them in the hamper, and as fast as he put one in, the other jumped out. This took some time. Then he carried the hamper up to bed with him, the kittens making frantic efforts to escape the while. And when at last he did get to bed, he had to get up again to let them out of the hamper, for they made such a frightful din no mortal could sleep. They finally elected to settle down on Mr. Neatby's bed, and in the morning one of them ungratefully scratched his nose because he happened to move when the kitten in question chose to walk over his face.

When at last he arose from very broken slumbers, the black kitten upset the shaving water and scalded its foot, and made a dreadful uproar, and the tortoiseshell, while investigating the mantelpiece, upset and threw into the grate a blue vase belonging to Mrs. Vyner.

In chapel on Sunday morning, Tod and Peter noted gleefully the long scratch on "old Stinks'" nose ("Stinks" being, I regret to say, the name by which Mr. Neatby was known among his pupils). And curiosity as to how he was getting on with his rapidly increasing family of cats consumed them. In the afternoon they walked up and down the road outside his lodgings for nearly an hour, but nothing did they discover; for Mrs. Vyner's windows were shrouded by white curtains, no one went in or out of the house, and all their loitering was not rewarded by so much as hearing a distant mew.

The fact was that Mr. Neatby had gone for a long walk to try and work off his irritation. That morning, while he was still at breakfast, Mrs. Vyner had appeared in his sitting-room, and somewhat stormily informed him that her "'ouse was not a 'ome for lost cats, nor never 'ad been." And she concluded her harangue as follows:

"I've 'ad gentlemen, masters at the school, for twelve year come Michaelmas, and some 'ave bin trouble enough, the Lard knows. With their football and 'ockey, and 'ot baths in the middle of the afternoon, and the mud on their flannings something hawful; but a gentleman as surrounded 'imself with cats in sech numbers I never 'ave 'ad nor never won't again, I 'opes and prays. And although it do go again my conscience to do it of a Sunday, I *must* ast you, sir, to take a week's notice from yesterday. For start a fresh week with sech goin's on, and cats a comin' by every post as it were, I can't; no, not if the king 'imself was to ast me on 'is bended knees."

In vain poor Mr. Neatby pointed out that, far from "surrounding himself" with kittens, they were thrust upon him he knew not by whom or from whence. That he had no intention of keeping any of them if Mrs. Vyner objected, and that it would really be extremely inconvenient for him to have to seek new rooms in the middle of the term.

Mrs. Vyner was implacable. "I'm very upset about it, too, sir," she answered, more in sorrow than in anger; "for I did think as 'ow I'd got a nice quiet gentleman, you not bein' given to them 'orrid games as is so dirty, nor wantin' an over amount of cookin'. But a gentleman as 'eaven appears to rain cats on like it do on you is not for the likes of me nor shan't be. And though I'm truly sorry as you should be so afflicted, I must ast you to leave my 'ouse, sir, next Saturday as ever is, and that's my last word."

It wasn't, not by a long way; for although Mr. Neatby reasoned, nay, even almost implored Mrs. Vyner to reconsider her decision, she would hardly let him get a word in edgeways, and remained unshaken in her desire that he should vacate her rooms. "'Ow do I know, sir," she asked again and again, "wot hanimals may be sent you next? My 'eart would be in my mouth every time the door-bell rang."

Truly, Tod and Peter had planned a fearful vengeance had they only known it. But they did not know it, and their unsatisfied curiosity was their undoing. On Monday morning at the riding school they arranged with Figgins that he was to leave the fifth kitten at Mr. Neatby's rooms that afternoon, just before afternoon school finished. The despatch of the hamper had been managed by a railway man, a friend of Figgins, whose cart started from a parcel-receiving office close to the riding school, and he delivered the hamper on his evening round.

Directly school came out, the twins decided to rush down to Mr. Neatby's rooms before lock-up, to ask some frivolous question about a paper he had set, and perhaps by great good luck be present at the unveiling of the end of the sending. All fell out exactly as they had arranged. Figgins took the parcel. Mrs. Vyner received it, addressed as before to "S. S. Neatby, Esq., M.A." (his real name was "Stuart," not "Stinks"), carried it grimly into his sitting-room, and laid it on the table. She removed all her own ornaments from the chimneypiece and sideboard, and then went downstairs and brought up all four kittens (poor Mr. Neatby had not yet had time to arrange for their painless destruction), and shut them up in the room to await their owner's return.

At ten minutes past five he hastened in, trod on one of the kittens as he entered the room, and struck a match to light his lamp. The kitten noisily proclaimed its injury, and the other three expressed their sympathy in similar terms. When he caught sight of the brown-paper parcel on the table he turned pale. The very feel of it was enough, and even before he had torn off the cover he was sure of its contents. Yes, in a common little bird cage was a fat, white kitten, and an uncommonly tight fit she was.

He did not attempt to let her out, though her position was plainly one of extreme discomfort, but stood with the cage in his hands, and the four mewing kittens about his feet, in so universally distrustful a frame of mind that he began to think that Mrs. Vyner herself was in the plot to victimize him.

The door was opened, and his landlady's voice announced: "Two young gentlemen to see you, sir."

Fresh colored and handsome, ruddy from their run in the cold evening air, square-shouldered and upstanding, Tod and Peter allowed their two pairs of candid blue eyes to travel from their master's angry face to his hands, from his hands holding the caged kitten to his feet, where congregated the rest of the sending, and then exclaimed in a chorus of genial astonishment: "Why, sir, what a lot of kittens you keep!"

Now, although he had been at the school three terms, no boy had ever ventured to call upon Mr. Neatby before. Other masters might occasionally ask boys to tea or permit an occasional call out of school hours to arrange about house matches, etc. But he had ever discouraged any familiarity whatsoever, and that Tod and Peter should dare to intrude upon him at such a moment seemed to him, as indeed it was, a piece of unparalleled impertinence.

"What do you want here?" he asked angrily. "It's after lock-up."

"Mr. Ord gave us leave to come," Peter said eagerly. "We don't understand this question, sir. Could you explain? What a noise those kittens do make, don't they?"

Now if Tod could only have refrained from looking at Peter, Mr. Neatby might have remained forever in the dark as to the mystery of the kittens. But, even as Peter spoke, Tod, unaware that the light from the master's lamp shone full on his face, winked delightedly at his brother, and in a flash Mr. Neatby connected their unexpected and unnecessary visit with those equally unwelcome visitants whose advent during the past week had entailed so much annoyance upon him.

Taking no notice of the paper Peter held out toward him, he laid the little cage on the table, and said very quietly:

"Now that you are here, you will perhaps kindly explain what you mean by sending all these animals to me."

"Us, sir!" the twins exclaimed breathlessly, and as usual in chorus—"Us!"

"Did you or did you not cause these five kittens to be sent to me?" Mr. Neatby asked again.

Dead silence.

As Tod said afterward, "It was one of those beastly yes or no questions that there's no getting out of."

"Did you or did you not?" Mr. Neatby asked again, a little louder than before, though even the kittens had ceased mewing and seemed to be listening. "But I know you did, and I wish to know further what you mean by a piece of such intolerable impertinence, and such wanton defiance of school rules."

"There's no rule about sending kittens, sir," murmured Peter, with the least suspicion of a giggle in his voice.

That giggle broke down the last barrier of Mr. Neatby's self-control. For full five minutes he permitted himself to thunder at those boys, finally bidding them take all five kittens away with them there and then.

"But we can't, sir; we *can't* take them back to the house," pleaded Tod. "Whatever would Mrs. Ord say?"

"Well, you must take them away from here, anyway, and what's more, you must give up the names of your confederates, that I may take proceedings against them for their unwarrantable interference with my privacy. Who were they, now? At once!"

"It's absolutely impossible for us to do that, sir," Peter said firmly, and Tod might have been heard to murmur something about "can't and won't."

"Then," said Mr. Neatby, "you will both come with me to the principal now at once."

The principal of that school is one of the youngest headmasters in England, and he would not be the success he is did he not possess a sense of humor. He partially pacified Mr. Neatby; he vigorously "tanned" Tod and Peter there and then, and during the remainder of the evening he laughed to himself more than once.

For the remainder of the term Tod and Peter found their comings and goings so perpetually watched and suspected by the "young brusher" aforesaid, that even the rapturous recollection of the success of their sending was somewhat dimmed. But it was not they who suffered most; to this day Mr. Neatby suspects of sinister intention anyone who so much as mentions kittens in his presence, and new boys always wonder why their schoolfellows are so anxious that they should mew in the chemistry lectures. They only do it once.

III
THE BOY THAT DIDN'T COME

During the first part of the next, the Easter, term the twins were so closely watched that their genius for mischief had small scope. Whereupon the authorities, finding them apparently absorbed in games and the general routine, relaxed their vigilance.

At the beginning of February the weather was mild and pleasant, with just enough rain to keep the footer ground in good order. But at the end of that fickle month there came a frost, the aggravating sort of frost that makes a field too hard for football and yet leads to no skating.

The never long dormant spirit of mischief in the twins awoke.

As usual, it was Peter who began it, though Tod was the innocent first cause.

Just after first lesson, as Tod was hurrying from one classroom to another, he met the principal in the corridor, who bade him ask his form-master to come and speak to him at a quarter past ten. Further down the corridor Tod met his twin, who instantly demanded what the "Pot" wanted, and on being informed, went upon his way.

Peter might have been seen to stop more than one schoolfellow as he went— the corridor was full of boys changing classrooms—and when he reached his own he delivered a message to the effect that the Head would like to see his form-master at ten-fifteen.

Peter's form-master, familiarly known as "Pig-Face," from a fancied resemblance to that animal in the matter of nose, is a testy man, much given to abusing his form and to the use of opprobrious epithets seriously reflecting upon the veracity of boys in general; so, on receipt of the Head's message, he knuckled Peter's head, called him a "shuffling little beast," set a complicated sum in discount for his form to wrestle with during his absence, and hurried away, fuming inwardly at the unreason of such a summons in the middle of morning school. When he arrived at the principal's room he found six other masters also in waiting, but the principal himself was not there.

It happened that that gentleman had met Tod's form-master three minutes after he had seen Tod, he said what he had to say there and then in the corridor, and dismissed the matter from his mind.

The seven masters waited in a grumpy group for ten good minutes, when, just as they had decided upon immediate departure, the principal himself rushed in and gazed in somewhat indignant astonishment at the assembled multitude.

It took nearly five minutes more to explain the situation, and the only boy whose conduct in delivering the various messages seemed not wholly inexplicable appeared to be Peter. For the principal good-naturedly came to the conclusion that it must have been Peter that he met, not Tod, and that Peter had misunderstood him.

Such a charitable view of Peter's conduct, however, could not last long, seeing that six angry masters rushed back to their respective forms to inflict lines upon six perfectly innocent boys, who were not slow to protest that the message was entrusted to them by another.

During the morning three young gentlemen from the Modern and four from the Classical received a summons "to the principal at twelve," and of course Tod and Peter were of the number, both looking so seraphically innocent that the principal was perfectly sure that it was "a put-up thing." In this instance the innocent suffered with the guilty, for Tod got five hundred lines as well as Peter. But they both agreed that to have so scored off seven "brushers" at one time was well worth the lines.

Three days afterward Tod's nose bled toward the end of morning school and he was dismissed to his house to clean up. As he raced along the corridor he noticed that the door of the little room into which the rope of the school bell descended was left open, and, peeping in, he discovered that Hooper, the trusty porter, was not within.

In far less time than it takes to write the words, Tod had rushed in, and the great school bell that dismisses morning school rang loud and clear over the peaceful playing-fields surrounding the school buildings, still humming with the busy life within.

Every boy and every master stopped short in what he was doing and looked at the clock. Those possessed of watches consulted them, shook them, listened to them, dubiously pressing them to unbelieving ears. And as the clocks in that school are by no means beyond reproach, being worked by a system of electricity that is, to say the least of it, capricious in its conduct, all came, not unwillingly, to the conclusion that morning work had indeed ended. Only the Head of the Modern, that man of iron endurance, whose whole scheme of creation seemed bounded by the exigencies of the Civil Service Commissioners, refused to believe that his watch was wrong, and continued to discuss the "directrix and eccentric" of a certain angle until it was really twelve o'clock; while one of the French masters, hailing from Geneva, proclaimed the unreliability of English clocks in general.

Meanwhile Hooper, who had gone down to the lodge to speak to his wife, could hardly believe his ears when his own sacred bell clanged, somewhat irresponsibly and gaily it is true, without his agency.

He rushed up the drive to discover the perpetrator of this extraordinary outrage, only to meet a throng of masters and boys streaming out into the playground full twenty minutes before the appointed hour.

Tod was nearly at his house by this time, and when he did arrive, hastened to the matron to descant upon the terrific hemorrhage that had occurred in his nose.

But Nemesis was never very leaden-footed where the twins were concerned.

"Other chaps," Tod remarked mournfully, "can break all sorts of rules and do no end of mischief and never get found out, but if we do the least little thing someone's certain to be down on us like a hundred of bricks, or else we're obliged to own up to save somebody else."

In this case it was the latter course that Tod had to pursue. The principal was exceedingly angry at such a wanton curtailment of the last hour of morning school, and gave it out in the afternoon that if the amateur bellringer did not disclose himself that very day, the whole school should stay in on the next half-holiday; and the frost had broken and football was in full swing once more.

Of course Tod sought the principal at the earliest opportunity and owned up.

When he appeared in the principal's room after afternoon school he made, it is true, a valiant effort to present himself with due solemnity, but his round face was absurdly chubby and cheerful, and when the principal looked up from the letter he was writing to see who the intruder was, he sighed deeply.

"You again, Beaton!" he exclaimed wearily. "So it was *you*, was it, who rang that bell? What on earth did you do it for?"

"My nose bled, sir...." Tod began eagerly.

"What had your nose to do with it?"

"Everything, sir. I was sent out of class...."

"Sent out of class?" the principal repeated sternly.

"Because I made such a mess," Tod hastened to add; "and the little door was open—and so I rang the bell."

"Beaton, when will you cease to play these senseless and annoying tricks? Your folly caused six hundred boys, to say nothing of the masters, to lose twenty precious minutes. If I punished you as you deserve, you ought to stay in for twenty minutes each day for six hundred days...."

Tod gasped.

"But I won't do that. Instead, you must do a thousand lines, to be given up by the end of this week. I shall not cane you, as I have no doubt you would infinitely prefer it."

A good many boys assisted to write those lines, and the impost was given up at its appointed time.

Hockey leagues were on and Peter was playing in his house team. On the morning of the last practice before an important match, he acknowledged so barely bowing an acquaintance with certain French idioms beloved of the French master—for was he not their author?—that Peter was told to stay in after morning school and learn them.

Peter did nothing of the kind; on the contrary, he went out at the usual hour and played hockey with his accustomed vigor, with the result that the French master sent for him that afternoon to know why he had not done as he was told.

Peter pleaded "a very important engagement," and, on being pressed to disclose the nature of that same, as usual answered quite truthfully. The French master, not unnaturally exasperated, forthwith reported him to the Head of the Modern, with the result that Peter was hauled up and bidden to stay in on the next half-holiday; the very half-holiday on which his house was to play its bitterest rival.

During the remainder of that term he got into several rows with his form-master, and Tod was equally unlucky, so that by the time the Easter holidays arrived both boys were quite ready for them and left school vowing vengeance on their persecutors.

Their parents were in India, so they went to spend the holidays with a jolly young bachelor uncle, who was an ardent fisherman and carried both the boys off with him for three weeks' peel-fishing in a remote village in North Wales. He was also of a literary turn, that uncle, and took with him a box of books to enliven their evenings: lots of Kipling and Stevenson, and amongst the latter the "Life and Letters." He read aloud the "Thomas Libby" incident, where Stevenson and certain kindred spirits roused a whole neighborhood to excitement by constant inquiries as to the whereabouts of one "Thomas Libby," who existed only in his creator's vivid imagination. That of the twins was immediately fired by an ambition to go and do likewise.

The incident, or rather series of incidents, to which the non-appearance of Mr. Libby led up, enchanted them. They chuckled over the mysterious Thomas for a whole day, but it was not till evening, at bedtime, that Tod whispered to Peter how, like "Sentimental Tommy," he had "found a way."

Sitting on the side of his bed, he announced gleefully: "Tell you what it is, Peter, we'll be a parent! A parent with a delicate kid! And we'll write long-winded letters in scratchy, small handwriting, you know, like the masters write...."

"But," Peter interrupted excitedly, "how are we to get the answers? It wouldn't be any fun if we didn't."

"The answers," Tod replied calmly, "will come to the post office here, where we're living, you juggins! You bet there'll be answers. They're awfully keen after the oof at the good old school. Why, they scent a new boy a mile off. He shall go into old Pig-Face's house, just to pay him out for all his beastliness to you, and I'll pester the Head about him and his delicate chest, and all that sort of rot that parents *do* write, don't you know."

Peter gasped. "But how can he 'go' into anybody's house if there isn't a him to go?"

"What an ass you are, Peter! *Was* there a Thomas Libby? And how many people's houses was he going to, pray?"

"Go on," said Peter humbly, "go on."

"The parent's name," Tod announced proudly, "is Theopompus Buggins."

"Theopompus!" Peter echoed dubiously. "It doesn't sound very real somehow—and is the kid to be young Theopompus?"

"No," said Tod firmly, "*his* name is Archibald, and Mr. Buggins is his uncle."

"I thought he was to be a parent," Peter objected in a dissatisfied voice.

"Well, an uncle is a sort of parent; probably the kid's an orphan."

There was silence for a minute while Peter digested this view of the matter. But still he was not quite satisfied, for presently he said: "Tod, would *you* believe in anyone called 'Theopompus Buggins'?"

"Well, no, I'm not sure that I would," Tod admitted. "Why?"

"D'you believe the Head will?"

"I never thought of that."

"I think," Peter suggested beguilingly, "that we had better have a commoner name, don't you?"

"P'r'aps we had," Tod sighed. "Let's have Jones—Theopompus Jones, now."

"Jones is all right," Peter allowed graciously, "but I don't fancy Theopompus much, it's such a peculiar name."

"It's a splendid name," Tod exclaimed huffily, "but of course if you think it's too uncommon he can be 'T. Jones, Esq.,' or 'John Jones' if you insist upon it. How would you like 'Peter Jones'?"

"T. Jones will do spiffingly," Peter answered with some haste. "*We'll* know his name is Theopompus right enough, and it don't matter a hang to them whether he's Theobald or Theophilus or anything; but I say, Tod, must he be an uncle?"

"Yes," Tod replied firmly, "he jolly well must, and, what's more, he's got to be going to Injia just as term begins. We'll look out the sailings in uncle's paper and choose his ship. He'll just get there in the hot weather, but that can't be helped."

The twins were well acquainted with the whereabouts of "sailings" in the papers, as most Anglo-Indian children are.

"Why, you've planned it all, Tod," Peter said admiringly. "How'll you do about the writing?"

"I shall write as like old Stinks as possible, that niggly, scrabbly sort of writing, *you* know."

"By Jove! So you can—that'll be all right. Parents and people call that sort of writing 'scholarly,' but if we did it they'd say we were beastly illiterate or something."

"What I like about a scholarly handwriting," said Tod thoughtfully, "is that no mortal can tell whether the spelling's right or not. When I'm once through the Shop I shall always write a scholarly hand and not bother about spelling and that any more."

"Boys," a voice called from the next room, "you get to bed and don't keep jawing all night."

It would not be fair to disclose the exact spot in Wales from which that anxious relative, Mr. T. Jones, indited his first letter to the headmaster of the Public School which reckoned Tod and Peter among its pupils.

"There are several L's in the place where he dwells,

And of W's more than one."

but it is impossible to be more explicit than this.

The Principal of Harchester School was at breakfast in his hotel at the seaside when a letter marked "urgent" and "if away please forward immediately" reached him. He turned it over thoughtfully before opening it, for he thought he recognized the handwriting of one of his masters (familiarly referred to by Tod and Peter as "old Stinks"), a science master, much given to drawing his attention to various details by means of lengthy epistles.

"What in the world can Neatby want now?" he wondered, "and in the holidays, too; it really is a little too bad!"

On opening the letter, however, he found that it was not from Mr. Neatby, and set himself forthwith to decipher a missive in which the margins were clear and spacious as the writing was small and obscure. Yet it had the air, so the principal remarked to himself, of being the letter of an educated man. Tod had played the "scholarly" game with entire success.

The letter was as follows:

"DEAR SIR,

"I am desirous that my only nephew, Archibald Jones, aged thirteen years and six months, should be enrolled among the pupils of your famous seminary at the commencement of the summer session. But before placing him under your benignant charge there are several points upon which I am desirous of enlightenment. Certain friends have recommended to me the house of one Mr. Mannock, but from other sources I have gathered that he is a man of somewhat violent temper, sometimes almost abusive, in his intercourse with the boys. Is this so? Because, if it is, I shall require to seek some other house in which to place my nephew, an orphan of extremely sensitive disposition, with a weak chest. It is possible that the accounts I have heard of Mr. Mannock's violence may be exaggerated, and I should like Archibald to enter his house unless you especially warn me against it. I wish my nephew to be entered upon the Classical side, as I am given to understand that boys are less overworked in that department than in that where they prepare for the Army. And as his delicate chest will prevent my nephew joining in the rougher sports of his contemporaries, I would suggest that one of the younger masters should be told off to take Archibald for a walk every fine day, as, of course, a certain amount of fresh air and exercise is essential. He must not be placed in too high a class, as owing to illness he has not been able to make such rapid progress in his studies as his robuster contemporaries.

"Any information that you can afford me—and as early an answer as possible, for I am leaving England at the beginning of May and wish to see my dear nephew comfortably settled before I sail—will greatly oblige

"Yours truly,
"T. JONES."

Tod had written "yours turly," but was corrected by Peter, who, if he had less sense of style, was fairly dependable where spelling was concerned.

Now the postmistress, their landlady, found her household duties so much increased by the presence of her lodgers that she was fain to depute her official cares to her daughter, Katie, a damsel who greatly admired the good-looking twins. And when they confided to her that if a letter came addressed to "T. Jones, Esq." it really was for one of them, she asked no questions, required no further information, but, concluding that it was only a part of their mysterious charm to receive letters in a name other than their own, promised to guard the same should it come, without pointing out to anybody that just then no person of the name of Jones was residing at the post office.

The letter came in two days and ran as follows:

"DEAR SIR,

"I enclose the entrance form to be filled up by any parent or guardian desirous of placing a boy at Harchester School. With regard to the house in which you wish your nephew to board, Mr. Mannock's is, as I hope are all our houses, entirely satisfactory. But if your nephew is, as you imply, a delicate boy, I would suggest that he should be placed in one of the smaller boarding-houses, as he would then receive more individual attention than it is possible to bestow in a house where there are some fifty boys. I have asked the bursar to send you a prospectus, in which you will find the names and addresses of all the masters in the school who take boys; and lest the house you select should be already full, I advise you to communicate with the master at your earliest convenience."

When Mr. Theopompus Jones in the dual shape of Tod and Peter received this missive they retired to a distant bridge, whereon they sat to read it, and they laughed so much that they nearly fell over backward into the river. They gloated over the very envelope. But later on, when their first glee at getting an answer at all had somewhat abated, they expressed disappointment that the Head had omitted to answer so many of their questions.

"You see," Peter cried indignantly, "what a shufflin' old hypocrite he is. You can't get a straight answer from him about old Pig-Face, and he knows what an old brute he is just as well as we do."

"Shall we send dear Archibald into one of the smaller houses?" Tod asked thoughtfully.

"No," Peter thundered. "He's going to old Pig-Face, and to no one else. Who knows but he may save some decent chap from going there? Let's write again to the Pot, it's such a lark, he answers so nice and quick. Why, there's over a fortnight more of the holidays; we can get a whole volume of his oily old letters by that time. I've always wondered how humbugs like him manage to grease up to one's people so, and for the life of me I can't see why now."

That night the twins again engaged in literary labors, much to their uncle's surprise, but he was an ardent bridge player, and, having found three like-minded anglers at the village inn, he was glad to leave his lively nephews so peacefully employed.

"Are you chaps writing a story?" he asked that evening as he departed to his bridge.

"Yes," "No," the twins answered simultaneously, then Tod answered with some decision: "No, Uncle Frank, we're writing letters, business letters, that's all."

"Dear me," their uncle replied, much impressed, and, having a peace-loving and incurious disposition, he asked no further questions and was soon contentedly playing a "no trumps" hand with conspicuous success.

A day or two later the headmaster of Harchester sighed gently as he found beside his plate at breakfast another bulky epistle from the anxious-minded Mr. T. Jones. This time that gentleman did not content himself with generalities; he made the most searching inquiries as to the disposition of the aforesaid Mr. Mannock.

After thanking the headmaster of Harchester for his "polite letter" (the headmaster raised his eyebrows as he reached this phrase), Mr. Jones continued:

"I fear that I cannot fall in with your suggestion of a private boarding-house for my dear nephew. In the first place it is too expensive, and in the second place I wish him to go into Mr. Mannock's house if you can satisfy me that he is of the considerate and forbearing disposition that a man placed in his responsible position ought to be. I am pressed for time, as I sail on May 1st for Bombay, and an early answer will greatly oblige.

"Yours truly,
"T. JONES."

Tod and Peter had the very greatest fun in filling in the form of application. They had long ago decided that the youthful Archibald was to enter on the Classical side, that he was destined for the Church, that his father was "deceased," but as to the late gentleman's profession they squabbled. Peter wanted Army or Indian Civil; Tod was in favor of Navy or Church; when Peter suddenly recollected that there were "lists and things" in most of the recognized professions and that an "inquisitive old buffer like the Pot would be certain to look him up."

Finally they decided that the deceased one had better be a "merchant." Peter wanted to add "prince," but Tod, the far-seeing, pointed out that such affluence would hardly coincide with an objection to one of the smaller boarding-houses on the score of expense.

Finally they despatched their entrance form "to the bursar," elaborately filled up in the scholarly handwriting of Mr. Theopompus Jones, the handwriting that so puzzled the Principal of Harchester by its haunting resemblance to that of one of his masters.

Again the Pot was prompt and courteous, and by return the twins were gloating over another letter, which, however, again disappointed them by its brevity.

"DEAR SIR (it ran),

"As your time in this country is indeed getting short, I would advise you at once to confer personally with Mr. Mannock as to whether he can find room for your nephew or not; for, in the event of his having no vacancy, you still may be enabled to place the boy in one of the other houses."

"Oh, the shuffler!" Peter shouted indignantly. "The quibbler! The sanctimonious humbug! *He* thinks he's diddled Theopompus Jones, does he? He'll find out his mistake before very long; it'll be Theopompus Jones has diddled *him*. I wouldn't trust that man with a bad halfpenny. He can't answer a straight question, that's what he can't do—and yet to hear him talk...."

"I say," interrupted Tod, "suppose they send in the bill, what'll we do?"

"You don't propose we should pay it, do you, you young ass?" Peter returned scornfully. "They never send 'em in till just before term, sometimes not till after. Don't you remember how the pater grumbled last autumn because it *didn't* come, and he wanted everything settled up before he sailed?"

"So does Mr. Jones want it all settled before he sails," Tod remarked gaily. "He ought to write to old Pig-Face to-night."

This the dual Mr. Jones did, and, as before, received an answer by return of post from Mr. Mannock, who, strange to say, had just one vacancy, and expressed his willingness that Archibald Jones should fill that same. And Mr. T. Jones, refraining from further researches into the character of Mr. Mannock, wrote with his own scholarly hand, or rather hands, a letter which announced the pending arrival of Archibald.

By this time the holidays were nearly over, and the twins began to be somewhat anxious as to the termination of Mr. Jones' correspondence with the authorities at Harchester School. But their good genius did not desert them at the last moment, for just the day before they left Wales, when they were at their wits' end for a satisfactory ending to the episode, they came across the "List of Members" of their uncle's club; and, idly turning over the leaves, Tod found that there were no fewer than thirteen members of the same surname as the anxious uncle of their creation and three of them had "T" for their initial. Instantly Tod's resource was stimulated, and he despatched three letters in the most scholarly of handwritings to his headmaster, to Mr. Mannock, and to the bursar respectively, announcing his immediate departure for London and requesting that all future communications might be addressed to him at the club in question.

In his letter to Mr. Mannock, he informed him that Archibald would be sent one day earlier than that given for the return of the other boys, as he, Mr. Jones, would be so much occupied in arrangements for his voyage that he would be unable to give the boy the careful supervision his sensitive disposition and delicate health demanded.

"We shan't see their pompous old letters and bills and things," sighed Peter, "but it will liven up the Jones fraternity at uncle's club—it's a good thing he's not going back to town just yet, or he might hear something—and Pig-Face will simply raise Cain when that precious Archibald mysteriously disappears. We're sure to hear about that, anyway; two of his chaps are in my form, jolly decent chaps they are, too."

"Mind you never *ask* anything about it," said Tod warningly. "They might suspect something, and if we were ever found to have had any hand in this we'd be sacked, sure as a gun. We've had our fun and now we must jolly well keep it dark. By the time it's all finished I should say both the Head and old Pig-Face will have done their thousand lines apiece, shouldn't you?"

"Curious thing that fellow never turning up, isn't it?" one of the "decent chaps" in Mr. Mannock's house remarked to Peter, some three days after term had begun. "Pig-Face is in an awful stew about it—afraid the boy's been murdered or something."

"What boy? What d'you mean?" Peter asked innocently. "Who hasn't come back?"

"No one hasn't come back; it's a new chap hasn't turned up at all. Both he and his people have mysteriously disappeared, vamoosed, vanished! Awfully funny thing. There's no end of a fuss."

"P'r'aps he changed his mind at the last minute," Peter suggested. "P'r'aps he heard something about old Pig-Face and funked it."

"I don't know," said the other. "Old Pig-Face looks awfully worried. Shouldn't wonder if we had detectives down, and all sorts of games."

Peter looked thoughtful for a minute, and then, to the astonishment of his friend, who was really impressed by the enigma, doubled up with uncontrollable laughter.

The assistance of Scotland Yard, however, was not called in; for, on writing to the Bishop and Admiral given as references by Mr. T. Jones (boldly lifted, address and all, from "Who's Who," by the ingenious Tod), the headmaster of Harchester received an emphatic disclaimer from each of these gentlemen of any knowledge of any such person. Moreover, an inquiry at the post office of the Welsh village from which Mr. Jones' letters were dated only elicited the laconic response of "Gone away—address not known."

Katie had received and faithfully followed her instructions.

Every Jones of the whole thirteen in that club was approached in vain, and inquiry at the shipping office only elicited the fact that, plentiful as persons bearing that patronymic appeared to be, no passenger of that name had sailed by that particular boat.

The authorities at Harchester came to the unwelcome conclusion that they had been hoaxed; and all that remained of the incident were certain letters, treasured, on the one hand for purposes of possible identification, on the other for more frivolous reasons.

"TONY"

Tony sat in the gutter, wondering what would be the coolest thing to do. The front doors of all the houses in the dull, quite respectable street, wherein he dwelt, were close shut, as were also the white-curtained windows, lest dust should blow in and sully these hall-marks of houses that possess a front "best room." The neighboring children were all away; some at the recreation ground, some to paddle their feet in the nearest approach to a river the town boasted—a little muddy stream about a foot deep at the best of times; now a sort of pea soup.

But on this August afternoon Tony felt too slack and too sticky to seek any amusement that necessitated a walk; so, having been thrust out of the back door by his mother, who was washing and wanted no boys "clutterin' round"—he strolled lanquidly to the front, quite sure that here, at any rate, he would be left in peace, as the dwellers in Eva Terrace never used their front doors except on Sundays.

Just then a man carrying a bag came running down the road, which was a short cut to the station.

"Here, youngster!" he shouted, throwing the bag to Tony. "Carry this for me, and I'll just do it! Run after me for all you're worth!"

Tony caught the bag dexterously and ran. He could run faster than the man, and was soon jogging on ahead of him. At the station Tony got sixpence for his pains, thrust it deep into his right trouser pocket, and walked soberly away.

Infinite possibilities were opened up by this unexpected windfall, and he had no intention of mentioning it at home. His people were poor, but not poorer than their neighbors; his brothers and sisters were all older than he, and in his case Benjamin's lot was not accompanied by the advantages with which it is generally accredited.

A lonely child was Tony, gentle and biddable enough, quick at his books, and happiest in his school hours, when people let him alone, and he succeeded in pleasing the clever, testy schoolmaster, whose life was embittered by a constant struggle with an overwhelming desire to whack the young demons who tormented him. He had been "summonsed" twice by irate parents; so now he restrained himself at the expense of his teaching powers and his nerves generally.

Tony stopped in the middle of the road and smacked his pocket.

"I'll go to the baths to-morrow morning," he said aloud, "and see them young nobs swim; it's only threepence before nine."

A great excitement—unshared, unmentioned—had lately come into Tony's life. Every morning for the last week, about eight o'clock he had watched for two boys who went by on bicycles with towels strapped on to their handlebars. One was quite a little boy, far less than Tony himself; the other bigger, and in his eyes less interesting; and in a few minutes after them came one for whom Tony had conceived the extravagant, unreasoning admiration children will sometimes lavish on somebody with whom they have never exchanged, or hope to exchange, two words; someone unconscious of their existence as they are the richer for that other's.

Everybody in Tony's locality knew the recruiting sergeant by sight: "Sergeant" who taught drill and gymnastics to all the "young gen'lemen" in the neighborhood. But Tony adored him, not only because he was so tall and good looking—and Tony was strenuously certain that it is a goodly thing to be upstanding and to have broad shoulders, instead of the champagne-bottle variety carried by his brothers and their like—but because he knew that the sergeant wished him well; inasmuch as that he, even he also, was one of the hundred and fifty odd boys in the parish schools of St. James's. For now that the war fever was somewhat abating, now that Sergeant himself had come back from the front that he might send more soldiers out there, he had offered to drill the boys in St. James's schools twice a week for love. And it could not be arranged.

The authorities, while granting the utility of algebra and French to those in the seventh standard, who were presently to form the bulk and bulwark of the nation, saw no good reason why an attempt should be made to give them straight backs and broad chests. So Sergeant, who loved his country, and was, in his way, something of a philanthropist, sighed and swore, and "put the question by."

But Tony, who had heard the subject canvassed, and listened to the lamentations of the boys, was filled with a passion of gratitude, which found no expression save in a constant hanging round corners to see his idol pass.

———

Tony sat on his bed naked, in a patch of moonlight, admiring his own legs.

"My body be whiter nor theirn," he said to himself, and indeed, his limbs looked radiantly fair in the mellow light. "But my arms beant so 'ard as 'is'n for all 'e be such little chap," he continued, pinching the soft flesh of the upper arm in a dissatisfied way.

Tony was too excited to sleep just yet—such a great deal had happened in the last two days. In all his ten years he had never felt as he felt now—and yet, from an outsider's point of view, what a little thing it was!

The day before he had gone to the swimming bath, intending just to watch. It was empty, save for Sergeant and the two boys who went with him every morning. The water looked so clear, and there seemed so much room in the big bath, that Tony undressed and went in.

He paddled shyly about in the shallow end, admiring the two boys, who dived off the spring-board and the pulpit and swam under water, while Sergeant roared directions at them, and flung them head over heels in the deep end, in a fashion that filled Tony with surprise.

The big boy was practising side-stroke, when the little one, whom Sergeant, for some reason or other, called the "swashbuckler," swam down the bath toward Tony, remarking cheerfully:

"You'll get rheumatism if you paddle so. Shall I show you the first exercise?"

He was such a little boy, but he swam like a frog. His square, freckled face was so friendly that Tony forgot that he himself was an "oik," and therefore his sworn foe, and said, "Please, sir!" in the meekest of tiny whispers.

"You must kneel on the edge further down, and let me chuck you in," was the next command—and Sergeant stopped in the very middle of a shout to chuckle and whisper:

"Blest if the swashbuckler isn't giving a swimming lesson on his own account!"

And now Tony sat on the edge of his bed and remembered two wonderful mornings, and pondered what it could be that made that friendly little boy so different from all the other boys he knew. And through all his thinking, like the refrain of a song, sounded a sentence he had once heard at Sunday school. He could not remember the whole of it; but five words seemed to batter at his brain as though demanding instant comprehension and attention—*"The temple of your body."*

Tony nodded as though in answer to a spoken word. He pictured Sergeant cleaving the water with his long arms, the muscles standing out on his white shoulders.

"I s'pose," said Tony softly, as if in answer to that unseen, persistent voice, "some folks 'as temples for bodies, and some folks 'as on'y tin churches, or, so to speak, a public.... I'd like a temple myself for ch'ice."

He was not very sure what a temple was, but in a vague way he *was* assured that it was something large and beautiful; and his conception was helped out by hazy recollections of Sunday school and Solomon, and thoughts of a building spacious and white.

"There used to be a free night," he continued, reverting again to the actual, "but the Corpeeration stopped it—I wonder w'y? It's tuppence after six, that's a shillin' a week—'ow can pore boys get that?—an' I promised 'im as I'd learn the others w'en I could get a chanst, when he's learned me...."

Tony's voice faltered, he was getting sleepy. He gave his smooth white arms another stroke, slipped into his nightshirt, and got into bed.

"E've give oi a shillin' to pay for four more mornin's, till 'e do go away," he whispered ecstatically as he laid his head on the pillow, and Tony fell asleep.

That evening Tony's elder brother "Earny," who cleaned bicycles, and was 'prenticed to a dealer in the neighborhood, wanted his Sunday necktie, for he purposed to "walk out with his young lady." He ran upstairs to the room he shared with Tony and another brother, to find the little boy fast asleep, worn out by unusual exercise and varied emotions.

Earny could not find his tie, and on lifting Tony's trousers to see if by any chance it was hidden beneath them, a shilling rolled out of the pocket and finished spinning with a clang, just in the very centre of the patch of moonlight where a quarter of an hour earlier Tony had decided that he, at all events, "would 'ave a temple for ch'ice."

"'Ullo!" thought Earny to himself, "where did that kid collar a bob? 'E bin a'ter no good, I'll be boun', so secret-like and sayin' nothin' to nobody. Serve 'im right if I buys some smokes with 'un;" and Earny departed quietly, without having fulfilled his original intention of waking Tony that he might look for the missing necktie.

At nine o'clock the following morning Tony still lay upon his bed, wide-eyed, white-cheeked, with blank despair writ large upon his face. Breakfast was over long ago, his family had all departed to their daily work; his mother was ironing in the kitchen, he could hear the bump of the iron as she slammed it on the table; the bedroom could wait till one of the girls came in at dinner-time, so no one interfered with Tony.

He knew that it was his brother who must have taken the shilling—the precious shilling that had meant so much to him. He knew that he had no redress, no one would believe him if he told them how he came by it, and in his utter misery he was too poor-spirited even to think of reprisals. His whole imagination centred round the dreadful certainty that Sergeant and the little gen'leman and the little gen'leman's brother would think him a fraud. For a brief space the sun had shone out on his drab life, discovering hitherto undreamt-of colors in the landscape, but now....

"I can never watch for 'em no more," he said, with a hard, tearless sob.

Presently he stood out on the floor and shook his nightshirt about his feet; he dressed quickly, and did not even wash his face as he was wont to do.

"'Tain't no use for the likes of me to try," he said bitterly.

Then he went to his brother's drawer and stole the bundle of cigarettes he found there, and went out and smoked under the railway bridge till his body was as sick as his heart.

A SQUARE PEG

"I told him plainly beforehand that if he did not get a scholarship this term he must go into business. He has not won a scholarship, and, situated as you are, any other course would be absurd."

Uncle Henry shut his mouth with a snap, while he stared fixedly over his sister's head that he might not see the pleading in her eyes as she said timidly:

"But fourteen is so young, Henry, and Rodney is so small for his age———"

"I fail to see that his size has anything to do with it; and you, Felicia, must learn to face things as they are, not as you would have them. If you defer for one moment the chance of Rodney's making his own living, you are doing an injustice both to him and to his sisters. Pardon my plain speaking, but he is the son of an exceedingly poor widow and must be dealt with accordingly."

Through the open windows came the sound of a boy's laughter and the ring of a smartly struck cricket ball. Uncle Henry waved his hand in the direction of the sound, saying:

"There, you see; that's what his education at present amounts to; he's a pretty bat, and doubtless looks forward to a life all flannels and cider-cup and yells of admiration when he makes a few runs; the sooner all that nonsense is knocked out of him the better."

"But Rodney is not idle, Henry," his mother pleaded; "his form-master and the Head both speak well of him and say that he has a very good chance next year, although he has missed this; you know the exam. came on just after his father's death, when the boy was dreadfully upset."

"I have made you an offer, you may take it or leave it. You can put him into one of my businesses; there will be no premium, and I'll pay for his board at a thoroughly good boarding-house I know of in Mecklenburg Square, where he will be well looked after. In the meantime you must try to let this house, and then you can come up and live in the suburbs, and he can live with you and go to business every day by train; the little girls can go to a High School. With the many claims I have upon me, this is all that I can do, and I must serve you in the way that seems best to me."

Uncle Henry sat down and took up the newspaper in token that the subject was thoroughly threshed out. He had gone into business at fourteen, and now at little past thirty had a house in Grosvenor Gardens and a "place down the river." He had married at six-and-twenty, "going where money was." The names of his two sons were down for Harrow, while his wife already talked of the time when she should "present" their baby girl. He quite acknowledged that it was his duty to help his sister now that the collapse of those Australian banks had practically beggared her; but there was at the back of his mind a lurking satisfaction that the way he had chosen should be one calculated to destroy those castles of tradition her husband had been so fond of building. It was a perpetual annoyance both to his wife and to himself that Rodney and his sisters should be so very different in appearance from their own children; that, clean or dirty, these children without a sixpence should so strongly resemble the old family portraits that his brother-in-law's ridiculous will forbade to be sold; that they should in speech and bearing so unmistakably be gentlefolk, and yet be his own sister's children seemed to him a proof of nature's ineptitude.

To be sure he and Felcourt had been on friendly enough terms, but he had always—though through no fault of Felcourt's—been conscious that his brother-in-law and his ancestors for generations belonged to a class which only of late, and that not altogether with enthusiasm, has opened its doors to successful men of Uncle Henry's stamp.

Rodney's mother went and stood by the open window. The active white figures flying between the wickets on the wide lawn seemed all blurred and indistinct, and she lifted her slim hand to her throat to still its throbbing ache; she was not a strong-minded woman. All she had asked of life was the power to make folks happy, and to be loved; and hitherto her desire had been generously fulfilled. Married at eighteen to a man who, taking her out of somewhat sordid and uncongenial surroundings, made her queen of a household where gaiety and good manners had been vassals for generations, she readily adapted herself to the new atmosphere, and became a sweet-voiced echo of her husband, and for fourteen years was absurdly happy. Then Rodney Felcourt died, and six months afterward came the collapse of the Australian banks.

Uncle Henry had a way of carrying through any course of action he had determined upon, and by the beginning of October his nephew Rodney found himself taking his exercise in the Gray's Inn Road instead of in the playing-fields at school. The change of life was so radical and so sudden that the child hardly understood what had happened. Like the old woman in the nursery rhyme, he was forever exclaiming, "This be never I!" in melancholy astonishment. He was learning to tie up parcels, he stuck on endless quantities of postage stamps, and occasionally addressed a few envelopes for one of the typists. He did what he was told as well as he could, the day seemed endlessly long, and by evening he was so tired that he went to bed soon after the seven-o'clock dinner. A young boy for his age, he was quite unprecocious and unformed; hitherto his place in the universe had been clearly defined and not difficult to fill; to do well in his form, thus pleasing the "mater" and his form-master, to be "decent" to his little sisters at home, and "jolly" with the chaps at school, to be good at games and get into the "house" eleven, and to be absolutely "straight" in word, deed, and across country—such was Rodney's conception of the whole duty of boy, and he had acted up to it with considerable success. Now, life was not only complicated but unintelligible, and he was too bewildered even to rebel against a fate that kept him tying up parcels indifferently well when he felt that by all the ordinary standards of conduct he ought to have been writing Latin verses.

Every Sunday he wrote neat, stilted little letters to his mother, which informed her that he had been to church at the Foundling, was going for a walk in the afternoon, that he was well and hoped that she was well, and that he was her very loving son. Felicia crushed the paper against her cheek in the vain attempt to extract from it something real and Rodney-like. She thought of the school letters last term, how full of life they had been, how numerous the requests they contained! Rodney never asked for anything now, and she knew that the boy was holding himself well in hand lest any part of the truth might hurt her.

At the end of October, Cecil Connop came back from Paris. His arrival was announced in all the papers, for he was of some importance in literary circles; his great ability was acknowledged on all sides, the more freely that he was something of a failure. Though his work was widely read and appreciated by cultivated people, he was not popular. His appearance was quite ordinary, and he made no attempt to resemble any historical personage. He abhorred advertisement, considering that his published writings had no sort of connection with his private life. His readers were quite ignorant as to whether he had a mother or not, and his personal friends suffered under no apprehension that their loves or their bereavements would figure, flimsily disguised, in his next book. His rooms in Jermyn Street had never been photographed, and only his servant knew whether he liked his bath hot or cold. The fact was that Cecil Connop kept one face for the world and quite another for the old friends who loved him—a proceeding so out of date among literary people as to be almost medieval. But it has its advantages for such as like curtains to their windows. According to his own account he never had any money, and was, when in England, in hourly danger of Holloway Jail; but he paid his card debts and never seemed to lack any of the things that go toward making life pleasant.

Felicia's letter announcing little Rodney's apprenticeship was a great surprise to Cecil. He had, of course, heard of her serious losses, but he knew that her brother was a wealthy man and "people always manage somehow"; that in this case they hadn't "managed" came upon him with quite an unpleasant shock.

For some reason which she would not define even to herself, Felicia had not asked any of her friends then in town to look up Rodney. She was absolutely certain in her own mind that he had no business there, but circumstances were too strong for her, and she dared not offend Henry. When she read in the paper that Cecil had returned to town she felt distinctly relieved. Here was an understanding person who would ask no questions and could be depended upon to give a faithful account of the child.

Cecil wrote at once to Rodney asking him to lunch at his club on the following Saturday, and to Felicia, to say how pleased he would be to do what he could for him while he was in town.

Rodney sat on the edge of his bed, too tired to undress. His flannels and "sweater" were spread on the pillow, and from time to time the boy laid his face down on them, inhaling the clean, woolly smell. He had of course never worn them since he came to London—Uncle Henry had not thought it necessary to make any arrangement as to how Rodney should spend his Saturdays—yet the sight of them comforted him. He was beginning to employ that saddest of all philosophies, that nothing can take from us the good times we have had. He had eaten hardly anything all day, and the ache in his throat was well nigh intolerable. His door opened, and the maid announced: "A gentleman to see you, sir. Said he'd come up here."

Cecil had come before his letter. As the open door betrayed the listless little figure with the scattered flannels the whole situation was revealed to him in a flash, and for the hundredth time in a not over well-spent life he cursed the folly which had rendered him so incapable of helping his friends in any material way. When Rodney realized who was his visitor, he simply flung himself bodily upon him, and Cecil Connop, who was tender-hearted and easily touched, kissed him and had been rapturously kissed in return before he had time to consider whether the boy would be offended or not. Then they both sat on the bed and for the first time for six weeks Rodney chattered. One of the boarders, a girl who did typewriting in Chancery Lane, passing his doorway, stopped and smiled as she heard the ripple of Rodney's laughter; she waited for a full minute, enjoying the unwonted sound, then passed on to her own room unaccountably cheered. People in that house were too busy and too tired to laugh!

When Cecil Connop got back to his rooms he sat and smoked for a long time before he wrote the following letter to Felicia Felcourt:

"To-night I have spent an hour with Rodney, and find him apparently well and cheerful. I cannot faithfully report upon his appearance, as it was candle-light and I did not see him very distinctly. He talked freely enough about you all at home, about his old school, about myself; but, when I come to think of it, said nothing about his business. You will, I know, pardon me if I ask you in all seriousness—is this necessary? The whole time I was with him I had a curious sense that he was playing truant and ought to be at school; and there is one thing that an expression in your letter impels me to say at the risk of being impertinent: no amount of money in the world is such a possession as the breeding you and his dead father have given your boy. Forgive this frankness and believe me that I feel with you the more keenly that I am so conscious of my own gross impotence to help."

On Saturdays Rodney left business at one, and on this particular Saturday flew back to "Meck" to change into his "Etons," when he hied him on the top of an omnibus to lunch with Cecil Connop at his club. When he was seated opposite to his host, that gentleman proceeded to examine him critically. The boy was unmistakably a gentleman: everything about him, from the long slender hands of which he was so unconscious, to the way he looked his companion straight in the eyes, proclaimed him to come of a race who had spent their days otherwise than in tying up parcels. Men passing in and out looked pleasantly at the pretty boy who was so plainly enjoying the unwonted experience; but Cecil noted that he was very thin, that after the first flush of greeting was past the little high-bred face was pale, and that there were black shadows under the long-lashed grey eyes. Moreover, although there was everything for lunch calculated to please a boy, he ate hardly anything.

"Are they decent to you at your place of business?" asked Cecil, carefully pouring cognac into his coffee.

"You see," said Rodney slowly, "I don't seem to know anybody...." Then, with a twinkle of amusement, "They call me a fool when I make mistakes, which is pretty often, and if I do things right nobody says anything."

During the next week or two Cecil made a point of seeing Rodney from time to time, and after each meeting he felt more and more convinced that the boy's health was failing. He did not complain, but the sedentary life was beginning to tell upon a constitution that had never been so tried. He began to stoop, and even with Cecil his laugh was by no means so ready or so frequent as it had been.

Felicia, although at first much comforted by Cecil's account of Rodney, longed after him as only widowed woman can long for her son; but she had promised her brother that she would not attempt to see the boy for three months lest it should unsettle him, and it only wanted three weeks of the stipulated time.

Rodney had not seen Cecil for a fortnight; he was out of town, but this Rodney did not know. It was Saturday, and a smell of onion curry pervaded the boarding-house, the Square garden looked hopelessly uninviting, and he felt that he could endure neither the one nor the other a moment longer. So he hied him to Pall Mall to see if he could catch a glimpse of his friend. A conspicuously forlorn little figure, he strolled slowly past the many clubs, when a man coming hastily down some steps stared hard at Rodney, and, fixing his eyeglasses more firmly on his nose, turned and walked swiftly after him.

"Felcourt! Felcourt! What are you doing here?" asked a sharp, nervous voice, and Rodney started violently as his house-master, "Fireworks Fenton," caught him by the shoulder and shook him.

"You young ass! Why didn't you write and tell me all about it?" said "Fireworks Fenton" an hour later, as he angrily thumped a tea-table in "Stewart's" till the cups jumped off their saucers. "We all thought you'd gone to another school, and here have you missed a whole term, and lost flesh and muscle, and forgotten everything you ever knew. I've no patience with you; it's preposterous, and must be put an end to at once! Give me your uncle's address and your mother's——" and "Fireworks" glared at Rodney through his eyeglasses, and Rodney sat swallowing uncomfortable things in his throat, while his heart felt lighter than it had been for many a long week. It was so good to be bullied in that particular fashion once more. Now he dared to look forward. He didn't in the least know how it was to be managed, but his old master had told him he was to come back to school next term, and *he* always got his own way even with the Head himself. "Fireworks" was not afraid of twenty Uncle Henries—"Worthy but mistaken, worthy but mistaken," he had muttered more than once during his late pupil's explanations. Rodney went with him to Paddington to see him off, and it was only as the train steamed out of the station that "Fireworks Fenton" recollected that he had omitted the special business he had come up to town to do. But he only frowned and muttered: "That ridiculous little Felcourt put it out of my head, but I'm glad I found him—glad I found him. What fools these dear women are! What fools! What fools!" and whenever he turned over a sheet of newspaper (of which he didn't read a line), he frowned again, exclaiming: "What fools!"

The particular fool Mr. Fenton had in his mind found two letters beside her plate on the following Tuesday morning. She knew both the handwritings, and gave a little sigh as she opened that from Rodney's house-master: it would be to ask how Rodney was getting on: he had always been fond of the boy, and she had told him nothing.

"You will, I hope, acquit me of frivolous interference," ran the letter, "in matters that do not concern me, when I tell you that I have seen Rodney and heard from him of the very great change it has been necessary to make in his life. I greatly wish that I had known sooner your reasons for taking him away from school, as I think one of the chief obstacles could have been, and still can be, easily removed. Dear Mrs. Felcourt, it is with considerable diffidence that I venture to ask you to do me a great favor, namely, to allow me to undertake Rodney's education; my one stipulation being that he should come back to my house. You know that where there are twenty to thirty boys, one more or less makes but little difference, and in becoming responsible for the school fees, I am doing no more than my headmaster did for me. My mother was left a widow with five children and very little of this world's gear. I am fully aware how much I shall be the gainer if you allow me to have Rodney, for, young as he is, he had a distinct influence upon that mysterious and fluctuating commodity, the 'tone of the house,' and I have not the slightest doubt that he will be able to make his own way by aid of scholarships, ultimately earning his own living nearly as soon as if he had remained in business.

"Forgive me where I have expressed myself clumsily, and believe me,

"Faithfully yours,
"REGINALD FENTON."

It was a long time before Felicia took up the other letter, which was from Cecil Connop, and of this one sentence stood out in letters of fire to the exclusion of everything else:

"I don't believe the boy's health will stand it, Felicia; come and see for yourself."

Felicia packed her smallest box and went.

When Rodney came back from business that evening Selina, the parlormaid, informed him that a lady was waiting in the drawing-room to see him. Selina, usually so grim, was all "nods and becks and wreathed smiles"; she liked Rodney, though he did "throw about his clothes something shameful."

He was very tired and his head ached, as it always did in the evening lately, but something in the maid's tone made him forget his weariness, and he raced up the stairs certain that only one lady could have produced such unwonted geniality on Selina's part. But he paused on the mat outside the door; suppose it should only be his aunt! She had never come yet, but she might, and how was Selina to know that he did not care particularly for his aunt?

The door opened suddenly from the inside.

"I *knew* nobody else would come upstairs like that. What were you waiting for, you dear goose?"—and Rodney's mother inspected her boy for herself.

Next day she went to see her brother at his office, and told him that she had decided to accept Mr. Fenton's offer. She rather surprised Uncle Henry, she was so decided and so cool; he did not know that Cecil Connop had got up two hours earlier than usual, in order to have plenty of time to fortify Felicia for the interview, only leaving her at the office door.

"Do you think he will refuse to have anything more to do with us?" she had asked timidly.

"He couldn't be so absurdly unjust," answered Cecil stoutly; "but, even if he were, you have Rodney to think of. It is a chance in a thousand; it would be worse than madness to throw it away. He's a square little peg, is Rodney; you'll never fit him into that hole."

Uncle Henry gave in quite graciously, though he was not best pleased. Had he but known it, he revenged himself upon Mr. Fenton for his interference by writing him a solemn letter of thanks, in which he spoke of his "generous, nay munificent offer." "Fireworks Fenton," very red and uncomfortable, rolled the letter into a ball and dropped it into his waste-paper basket, exclaiming:

"Pompous idiot!"

When Rodney went home his little sisters found him more delightful than ever, but he was reticent as regarded his experiences in London, describing it briefly as "a beastly hole."

On his return to school "Fireworks Fenton" sent for him the very first evening.

"A row already, Felcourt!" exclaimed his best friend in dismay.

But Rodney ran along the passage and knocked at the study door without any fears on that score. As he closed the door behind him it was the master who looked embarrassed, as he jerked out:

"I'm pleased to see you back, Felcourt. Remember that if you are in any way perplexed, or get into trouble ... or ... do you want any pocket-money, by the way?" and "Fireworks" bent anew over the letter he was writing.

"No, sir, I have the usual pocket-money, thank you; but please I would like to——"

"Now, Felcourt, don't you see that I'm busy? Go away, go away!"

"But please, sir——"

"I know perfectly well all the absurd and ridiculous things you would say, and I very much prefer that you should not say them. One thing *I* have to say, attend to your English prose! I have a distinct recollection that your spelling of English is revolting—positively revolting. Attend to it!"

A TWENTIETH-CENTURY MISOGYNIST

What a place to be in is an old library! It seems as though all the souls of all the writers that have bequeathed their labors to these Bodleians were reposing here, as in some dormitory, or middle state. I do not want to handle or profane the leaves, their winding sheets. I could as soon dislodge a shade. I seem to inhale learning walking amid their foliage; and the odor of their old moth-scented coverings is fragrant as the first bloom of those sciential apples which grew amid the happy orchard.—CHARLES LAMB.

I

Every Easter holidays the schoolmaster went back to Oxford. Head of a flourishing preparatory school in the north, a bachelor, absorbed in his boys, strenuous, matter-of-fact, he yet retained after some twenty years of monotonous grind a romantic affection for the dear city of his youthful dreams.

He always put up at the King's Arms, that ancient hostel with the undulating floors, where the ale is brown and strong, and the cold beef tender and streaky. On his very first day he hied him to a solitude he loved, paid his modest threepence, and mounted to a favorite haunt of his—the picture-gallery of the Bodleian Library.

It was always empty; it almost always is empty. Undergraduates know it not; artistic and intellectual residents appear to scorn its prosaic portraits of bygone poets and college benefactors, its humble curiosities. Visitors seldom trouble themselves to mount the few extra steps leading to it from the world-famed library below. But the schoolmaster loved to wander up and down the second gallery. He loved the double archway with the traceried roof, where the statue of William, Earl of Pembroke, stands in the centre, and the two wide bay windows are filled with pale stained glass, and one has a deep, comfortable seat.

As usual, the gallery seemed deserted, and the schoolmaster let the peace of its solitude slide into his soul, till his spirit was compassed about with a great calm. He strolled slowly through the gallery, his hands, holding his straw hat, clasped behind him. He always uncovered the instant he entered the little modest door in the corner of the great quadrangle that leads to so many wonders. Presently he reached the archway where he was wont to sit and dream.

With a start of surprise he discovered that it was already tenanted.

Under the portraits of Ben Jonson and Joseph Trapp, curled up in a corner of the deep window-seat, his muddy boots reposing on the sacred oak, was a boy—a small, thin boy in Norfolk jacket and knickerbockers, apparently

- 49 -

about twelve years old, who read absorbedly a popular illustrated magazine. He never looked up as the schoolmaster approached. Apparently he neither heard his footstep nor realized that the newcomer had paused to stare at him in speechless astonishment.

Amazement, accompanied by extreme annoyance, was the schoolmaster's predominant emotion. There seemed to him something incongruous to the verge of irreverence in anyone daring to read a modern magazine under the very roof of the building that contained so much of venerable scholarship.

It is true that the boy was perfectly quiet. Beyond the turning of his page, he made no sound of any sort, and the schoolmaster found himself watching this reader with a sort of dreadful fascination. He longed that the child should reach the bottom of his page and look up. He even gave a little cough to attract his attention. But the boy seemed absolutely unconscious of either the stranger's presence or his scrutiny, and read on unmoved, smiling occasionally at what he read.

The schoolmaster fussed to the end of the gallery, pausing at every window to look out over the roofs at the towers and spires of Oxford. Then he fussed back again along the other side, where the view consists of the grey-walled quadrangle, a veritable "haunt of ancient peace." The peace that had enveloped him on his first entry spread her wings and fled. Irritation and curiosity had taken her place, and as he reached the archway again he stopped and looked at the motionless little figure in the window.

The boy was no longer reading.

The magazine lay on the window-seat beside him. His knees were drawn up to his chin, his arms clasped about them, and he stared unblinkingly at the portrait of Abraham Cowley on the wall that faced him.

The schoolmaster walked round the statue of William of Pembroke till he, too, faced the boy. This time the child certainly glanced in his direction, but the glance was of the most cursory order, and wholly without interest. In an instant he had returned to his grave contemplation of the poet, and the schoolmaster might himself have been the statue of William of Pembroke for any interest he excited.

The boy was pale and thin-faced, with large, hollow eyes and a tall, wide forehead—a scholar's forehead, as the schoolmaster, accustomed for years to the observation of boys, had already noted. But what latent scholarship was displayed in the reading of that obnoxious magazine? And what business, the schoolmaster asked himself angrily, had a boy of that age to be boxed up indoors on a fine afternoon in the Easter holidays?

The schoolmaster was a conscientious man in the pursuit of his calling. From the very first he had taught himself to look upon boys as individuals. He loved them; he whole-heartedly wished them well. They were to him of most absorbing interest; but he liked to get away from them sometimes, and nowhere had he been able to pass so completely from his ordinary life of a hundred petty duties and anxieties as in the high solitude of that deserted gallery, set in the very centre of the scenes he held most dear, now spoilt and desecrated by this young interloper with his horrid modern magazine. Why on earth did he choose to come here?

The schoolmaster could bear it no longer. "Boy," he exclaimed, "why do you come and read here?"

Slowly the boy turned his melancholy eyes upon his questioner. "Because," he answered, civilly enough, but without any enthusiasm, "it is generally perfectly quiet here."

There was the faintest perceptible emphasis on the "generally," not so much impertinent as gently reproving. Having answered, he turned his eyes again upon the chubby, smiling countenance of Abraham Cowley, and silence fell upon them like a pall.

The schoolmaster was baffled, but more curious than ever. He was quite conscious of the implied reproach in the "generally," and he noted the absence of the courteous "sir" with which any properly constituted boy would conclude a remark made to an elder. But he could not feel that the boy had been willfully rude. He would try again. "May I ask," he said pleasantly, "why you are so fond of looking at the portrait of Abraham Cowley?"

Again the boy shifted his gaze from the smug charms of the poet to the worn and somewhat homely features of his questioner.

"I like him cos he's so good-tempered—in this one," was the brief reply.

The schoolmaster came and stood beside the boy, and looked at the portrait. Above it was another, also by Kneller, but representing him as thin and severe-looking.

"They're very different, aren't they?" the schoolmaster remarked. "You'd hardly think they were the same man, would you?"

"I expect," the boy said solemnly, "in the top one he's been married."

This startling supposition fairly took away the schoolmaster's breath. He racked his brains to remember all he had ever heard or read of Abraham Cowley, and couldn't for the life of him recollect whether he was married or not. It is not in the nature of a true schoolmaster to leave a youthful mind in the darkness of ignorance if he can be the bearer of a torch whose light may pierce that gloom, so he said: "I expect it was his political troubles that caused so marked a change in his appearance. Do you know anything about him?"

"No, but I like him."

"Shall I tell you about him?"

"No, thank you," the boy answered politely, but with firm finality.

He took up his magazine again, opened it, spread it upon his knees, and in one instant was absorbed in its pages.

The schoolmaster sat down on the window-seat and gazed alternately at the boy and at the portraits of Ben Jonson and Joseph Trapp above his head. Since he had been a little boy himself he had never felt so snubbed. He was wholly unaccustomed to be a cypher in the eyes of boys, and suddenly with devastating force there was flung upon him the conviction that he never saw a real boy at all—that the boys he saw were all carefully expurgated editions arranged to suit his sensibilities.

A wild spirit of enterprise seduced the schoolmaster. He felt himself as one who after long sailing in smooth, familiar waters suddenly sights an unknown and precipitous shore.

He had come to Oxford to get away from the boys he thought he knew. What if, at Oxford, he received real enlightenment with regard to a boy he did not know? The sunshine faded and the gallery grew dark. Outside, he heard the soft patter of a heavy April shower.

"You ought not to read in this light," he said suddenly, "you will hurt your eyes."

The boy looked up surprised at this fresh interruption, but he obediently closed his book: there is something almost irresistible in the commands of those accustomed to exert authority.

"Do you come here often?" asked the schoolmaster.

"Yes, whenever I've got threepence to get in."

"Has no one ever told you that when you are talking to an older man it is considered polite to say 'sir'?"

"No. I don't know many old men, nor men at all, for the matter of that."

"Why, Oxford is full of men."

"That may be. I don't know 'em. I only wish I did."

The boy spoke bitterly and his eyes were full of gloom.

"Don't you go to school?" this "older man" asked anxiously.

"No, I'm too delicate, so they say."

"Who teaches you, then?"

"A guv'ness. I say, do you think we *ought* to talk here?"

"I see no reason why not. This isn't the library, there is no notice enforcing silence."

The boy looked as if he wished there was. He sat perfectly mute, with his eyes fixed on the placid portrait over the schoolmaster's head.

"Wouldn't you like to come downstairs with me and see some of the curiosities in the library?" the schoolmaster suggested beguilingly.

"No, thank you."

Really it was most difficult to make any headway with this boy. But the schoolmaster possessed to the full the necessary perseverance of his craft, so he continued his catechism:

"Do your parents live in Oxford?"

"I haven't got any parents, they're dead."

"Dear me, how sad! With whom do you live, then?"

"Aunts."

Written words can in nowise express the snappiness with which the boy ejaculated this monosyllable. The schoolmaster felt unaccountably chilled and worsted, and silence fell upon them once more.

The black cloud had passed over the Bodleian, the rain ceased, and the sun shone out again. The boy swung his feet off the window-seat, put on his cap and picked up his magazine, and without a word of farewell, strolled nonchalantly out of the gallery, leaving the schoolmaster to exclaim when he had finally vanished, "Well, of all the curmudgeony boys it has ever been my lot to meet, there goes the most curmudgeony!"

II

Yet he found it difficult to dismiss the ungracious youngster from his thoughts. Next afternoon he sought the gallery again, but there was no little figure curled up in the deep window-seat. The poet Cowley smiled serenely, the gallery was deserted, dignified, reposeful as of yore: with all its mellow charm of faded coloring, that even the luminous stillness of that April afternoon could not burnish into real brightness. But the usual sense of pleasant well-being, and ordered peace, failed to enwrap the soul of the schoolmaster. Even as the day before he had found the presence of the reading figure in the window irritating and incongruous, so to-day he found its absence singularly disturbing. He walked once round the gallery, sat a few minutes looking at the portrait of Cowley and wondering what mysterious charm it held for the queer child who loved it, and so into the dear familiar irregular streets, where he scanned every boy who passed, in the hope of coming across his small acquaintance of the day before. He went every day to the gallery, but no boy was there. He almost gave up hope of ever seeing him again, but he did not forget; and when, eight days after their first meeting, he mounted to the gallery and saw the little figure crouched in the window as before, with a gaily covered magazine open on his knees, the schoolmaster's heart beat a little faster, and he hurried forward, exclaiming: "Where have you been all these days?"

The boy started at his greeting, looked up, and a smile of recognition changed his face so absolutely that the schoolmaster felt a queer tightening in the muscles of his throat.

"I don't get my pocket-money till a Friday," the boy explained. "I couldn't come before."

"Well, now you are here, let's have a chat together," the schoolmaster said genially. "We both like this place, let's tell each other the reasons why, and see if they're the same."

He sat down beside the boy, just out of reach of the muddy boots. The boy, his magazine still held open on his knees, surveyed his neighbor with dark, mournful eyes. Now that the smile had ceased to lighten his face, the schoolmaster was shocked at the sharpness of the thin cheekbones, the hollows and the blue shadows under the solemn eyes.

"I can't tell you why I like it," said the boy, "'cept p'r'aps because it's so quiet, no one ever talks here, and there's no women."

"But women can come here if they like," the schoolmaster objected.

"They never *do* like, not when I'm here," the boy exclaimed eagerly. "I've been here every week for months and months and I've never seen one."

"But why do you object to women?" the schoolmaster persisted. "We should be in a poor case without them, most of us."

"*I* don't object to them," the boy said wearily; "it's them objects to us, and they do talk so—talk and talk and talk about their sufferings."

"Sufferings?" the schoolmaster repeated.

"*You* know," said the boy impatiently, "women's sufferings and votes and things, and Parliament and injustice and that."

"Suffrage, suffrage, you mean suffrage!" cried the schoolmaster.

"It's all the same, that's what they talk about, and inferiority and that. One can't help being born a boy, can one?"

"*Help* it!" exclaimed the schoolmaster. "Why, who'd be born anything else if they had their choice?"

The boy's pale cheeks flushed. "Do you really mean that?" he asked eagerly.

"Of course I do. It's a glorious thing to be a boy who's going to be a man."

"*They* don't think so, they say it's much better to be a girl; they're sorry I'm a boy."

"Oh, come," the schoolmaster said chaffingly. "You can't expect me to believe that. They may say so in a kind of joke, but they don't really mean it."

"Do you know my aunts?"

"Well, no; but I expect they are very like other ladies, who often say what they don't mean."

The boy gave one scornful glance in the direction of the schoolmaster, lowered his eyes to the printed page, and was instantly absorbed.

The schoolmaster felt that he was dismissed. He had been weighed in the balance, and found wanting in sympathy and insight, a mere stupid looker-on at the outside of things. Five minutes ago the boy had welcomed him. Now, it was as though the child had risen with the royal prerogative, and closed the interview. The schoolmaster sighed deeply.

The boy looked up. His eyes were the color of a still pool in a Devonshire trout stream, brown, with olive-green shadows, suggesting depths unfathomable. The schoolmaster instantly seized upon the small concession, exclaiming: "I came here every day in the hope of seeing you again, and now that you are here, you sit and read. Don't you think it's rather unkind?"

The boy flushed hotly, and once more the transforming smile illumined his face as he said: "You came here on purpose to see me? Why?"

"Well, you see, I've known a good many boys in my time, and I thought you seemed a bit lonely...."

The hungry eyes devoured him, and the schoolmaster stopped in the middle of his sentence, for, like all Englishmen, he dreaded any manifestation of feeling, and the boy looked as if he were about to cry. His fears were groundless, however, for the child only said: "How many boys have you known?"

"Rather over a thousand, I fancy. You see, it has been my business to have to do with boys for over twenty years."

"Over a thousand boys—and I don't know one! How unfair things are, and beastly."

The boy looked enviously at the grizzled man who had known so many boys; and the man looked pityingly at this boy who seemed to have been somehow cheated of all that makes youth joyous.

"How is it you have no friends of your own age?" he said presently. "Why don't you beg your aunts to send you to school? You'd probably get stronger directly you got there, with the regular games and busy life."

"My aunts don't like schools. They say boys learn to be tyrants and bullies at school."

"Oh, do they? You couldn't have fifty tyrants in one place, or they'd be the death of one another, like the Kilkenny cats."

"My aunts say," the boy continued, "that I'm to be a result. I won't be a result. It's beastly to be a result. I'll be a policeman when I'm grown up. Just you wait. I'll stand outside Parliament, and if a woman comes near I'll carry her to jail. You see if I don't."

The boy spoke with such vindictive bitterness that the schoolmaster was shocked.

"I have no doubt," he said soothingly, "that your aunts have good reasons for many of their views. You cannot possibly judge of such questions for many years to come."

"You'd judge if you heard it all day long like I do," the boy retorted. "It's only here I get away from it. Here in this nice quiet with that fat, contented chap smiling at me; and now you've been and made me talk about it, so even *he* will know. You've gone and spoilt my place—it's too bad."

The boy looked as if he was really going to cry this time, and the schoolmaster felt dreadfully guilty.

"Tell me about your parents," he said hastily. "Do you remember them?"

"My father died before I was born, and my mother just after—she always was very unwise."

"My dear boy, you ought not to speak about your mother like that. You shock me."

"Well, *they* say so."

"If anyone was to say to me that my mother was unwise, I'd—I'd knock him down!" the schoolmaster exclaimed.

"P'r'aps you knew her?"

"Thank God, yes!"

"Ah, I didn't, you see—and I don't think I could knock Aunt Amabel down—she's very strong."

"Of course not, of course not," the schoolmaster said hastily. "I never suggested such a thing for a moment. I expect you misunderstand your aunts, and it is possible that they don't quite understand you."

The boy said nothing. He no longer stared at Cowley's portrait. He stared at the schoolmaster, and in his melancholy gaze was concentrated all the bitterness and disappointment of his twelve short years.

"Let us come out and walk by the Cher," said the schoolmaster.

The boy followed him obediently, and as they turned into Catharine Street, slipped his hand into that of his new acquaintance.

"Twelve years old," thought that worthy, "and he takes a fellow's hand. Poor little chap!" Aloud he said: "Boys generally take each other by the arm, you know."

Instantly his companion seized him by his, and arm in arm they sought the sheltered walk loved well by Joseph Addison.

III

After that they met every day in the quadrangle of the Bodleian by appointment, and together mounted to their favorite seat in the picture-gallery. The boy no longer read a magazine; instead, he asked questions—endless, anxious, exhaustive questions—as to the usual doings and habits of boys who lived with each other and were brought up by men. All his ideas on the subject were gathered from school stories, and in consequence were crude and chimerical in the extreme. It was undoubtedly a shock to him when this kindly friend of his frankly admitted that he had frequently caned boys, and that he was supposed to have "rather a heavy hand." And the schoolmaster was still more shocked at the bitterness of soul he discovered in this queer, quiet boy. He gathered that the aunts—generally spoken of as "they"—were ladies wholly absorbed in politics and every kind of movement for the emancipation of women, and the schoolmaster pictured them as members of the shrieking sisterhood, ill-favored and ill-dressed, oblivious of the fact that feminine political opinions do not necessarily march in elastic-sided boots. When the boy did condescend to mention one of his aunts by name it was always of "Aunt Amabel" he spoke. She appeared to be the guiding spirit of the trio, busy, strong, and energetic, spending what time she could spare from politics in the pursuit of all those games from which the unfortunate boy was debarred by lack of comrades, and the schoolmaster found himself thinking with quite unusual enthusiasm of the sister who kept house for him. At times he had regretted her exclusively domestic talents. Now he even began to share her serene conviction that women were, on the whole, so much superior to men that only the very foolish could wish to resemble them.

In the course of their long talks the schoolmaster had enlightened his companion as to what constituted, in his simple creed, the whole duty of boy; and so far as his ideals related to honor and courage and truthfulness, he found the child singularly receptive and responsive; but when he touched on the chivalry that should be shown to women, when he tried to arouse the protective instinct that is generally so deeply rooted and spontaneous in even the most rough and tumble average boy, he was met by blank incomprehension, or a veiled hostility that puzzled and depressed him. "If this," thought he to himself, "is the result of the feminist movement on the rising generation of men, God help the next generation of women!"

The men had come up, and the schoolmaster's holiday was nearly ended. In two days more he would need to return to his duties in the North, to look after the cricket pitches in the playing-fields, and to see that all was shipshape for the boys' next term. For the last time he met his sad-faced little friend in Catharine Street. This time they did not go up to the picture-gallery. It was a sunny day in late April, when Oxford seems to burgeon and blossom in a riotous ecstasy of youth and gladness. River and playing-fields were gay with lithe, flannelled figures, and everywhere the air was sweet with the scent of opening lilacs.

"We'll go on the river this afternoon," cried the schoolmaster when he spied the little figure waiting for him; "it's far too fine to be boxed up indoors. I'll take you in a Canadian canoe. You must sit very still, you know. You don't think your aunts would mind, do you?"

"They're in London. Aunt Amabel comes back to-night, but she'll be off again in a day or two; she's always going to meetings. I'm jolly glad she's been away this week; she might have wanted to interfere——"

"I don't think she would mind your coming out with me, or I wouldn't take you. You must tell her all about it this evening. I'll give you my card to show her, and you can explain how we met."

The boy's dark eyes were mutinous as he took the proffered card and put it in his pocket, but he said nothing. On the river in the bright sunshine the schoolmaster noticed how very ill he looked, and a great desire possessed this kindly soul to make things easier for the boy. The sight of the black shadows encircling the sombre eyes that should have been so bright with youth and hope decided the schoolmaster to do what he most hated doing— to interfere in another's affairs, where he had no possible excuse or even reason for so doing.

He walked back with the boy to his home, one of the large, ugly, comfortable houses "standing in its own grounds," that have sprung up on the outskirts of beautiful old Oxford: a house that looked excessively well-to-do and trim and neat. "Nothing of Mrs. Jellyby here," thought the schoolmaster.

"Shan't I see you again?" asked the boy in a husky whisper, as they reached his gate. "It'll be awful when you're gone."

"We'll see, we'll see," the schoolmaster said hastily. "I can't make an arrangement now. Good-bye, my boy. God bless you!"

The boy's wistful eyes were more than he could bear. The man turned hastily and walked away, nor once looked back at the watching figure by the gate.

Next morning he called upon Aunt Amabel about ten o'clock. The less conventional the hour, the more possible did he feel it might be to explain his errand. She was at home and would see him. The boy had evidently done his bidding. As he followed the maid from the drawing-room to the study, he prayed that some Pentecostal gift of tongues might be vouchsafed to him.

Aunt Amabel was seated at a large knee-hole table covered with papers. She rose as he came into the room and held out her hand. The business-like table, the litter of papers, was exactly what the schoolmaster had expected, but the lady was wholly unlike the lady of his dreams. Tall, well-dressed, good-looking, and by no means old, she made things harder for him by her welcome. "You are the gentleman who has been so good to Reginald? It is kind of you to call. I am most pleased to meet you. He is a somewhat unusual boy, is he not? We rather pride ourselves on his taste for old buildings, and things that do not generally appeal to boys."

The schoolmaster mumbled some vague politeness and seated himself upon a chair which faced the knee-hole table. Aunt Amabel's eyes were dark, like the boy's, but they were bright and lively, and she turned them now upon her visitor with full inquiring gaze.

"I came," the schoolmaster said bluntly, "to see you about your nephew. He is not well, and I think his state of health arises largely from the fact that he has no companions of his own age, nor suitable interests. Why don't you send him to school?"

As he spoke he was perfectly conscious that this self-possessed young woman was misjudging him, and the knowledge made him even less diplomatic than usual.

"We have never considered him strong enough for school life. He is an unusual child of difficult temperament. He would be extremely unhappy at school."

There was a superior finality in the lady's tone that roused all the fighting element in the schoolmaster. "He could hardly be more unhappy than he is at present," he said sharply. "I know that this must appear, as indeed it is, a piece of unwarrantable interference on my part, but, having become really interested in the boy, I could not reconcile it to my conscience to leave Oxford without warning you that if you persist in keeping your nephew away from the natural companionship, amusements, and employments of his age, he will wither away as surely as a plant withers when light and air are withheld from it. That boy will die."

He shook a thick forefinger at her, and the scorn died out of her eyes. The men who most countenance the woman's movement are seldom masterful. Aunt Amabel began to like this dictatorial man. It was a new, and not altogether disagreeable, experience to be rated.

"You have a school, haven't you?" she asked, sweetly.

The schoolmaster's dun-colored face crimsoned. "My dear young lady," he answered hotly, "if you imagine that I came to see you because I was touting for another pupil, pray dismiss the idea from your mind." This time it was Aunt Amabel who blushed. "I came because, knowing a good deal of boys, I feel sure that your nephew is delicate because he is lonely and unoccupied; he is a very boyish boy, a boy who needs the companionship of his own kind. You have an excellent preparatory school quite near here. Try for a term— see what it does for Reginald."

"To be quite candid," said Aunt Amabel, "we do not care for the training, mental or moral, that boys receive at the average preparatory school."

"Try one that's not average," he interrupted. "There are plenty of them, all fads and flannel shirts and girls thrown in. He won't learn anything, but what does that matter? It's health and youth and gladness that you want for him, and a normal point of view; at present that child's a perfect misogynist."

The lady started at the word, and at this critical moment her nephew came into the room. At first he did not see his friend of the Bodleian; when he did he stopped short, looking from his aunt to her visitor with puzzled, timid eyes.

"Reginald," said Aunt Amabel, "this gentleman says you are lonely and unhappy, and that you would really like to go to school. Is this so?"

"Yes."

The timid look faded from the boy's eyes to be replaced by one that was almost stern, so earnest was it.

"Why have you never said anything to me about it? You have never complained."

"What was the use?"

"But how could we know you were not happy if you never said anything?"

"He knew, without my never saying anything." The boy pointed at the schoolmaster, who sat with downcast eyes.

"So it appears," the lady said somewhat tartly, "although you seem to me to have said a good deal. That will do, Reginald; you may go."

But Reginald did not go. He looked at the schoolmaster, and he looked at his aunt. He took a step forward, exclaiming earnestly: "If you will let me be like other boys, Aunt Amabel, I won't be a policeman when I'm grown up; I'll give it up; I'll truly be something else." The boy spoke as one who promises to part with some long-cherished and imperishable ideal.

"Oh, child!" exclaimed poor, puzzled Aunt Amabel, "I can't imagine what you are talking about. *Do* run away."

"You see," said the boy sadly to the schoolmaster, "she never *can* understand," and he hastened from the room.

The schoolmaster rose. "Believe me," he said gently, "I do not want your nephew for a pupil. I'd far rather keep him as a friend—I don't mean to say that a master can't be a friend to his boys, but the relationship must necessarily be a little different, and it has been a pleasant experience to come across a boy under quite new circumstances. I wouldn't spoil it for the world."

Aunt Amabel looked down, and the schoolmaster noticed that her eyelashes were long and very black. "I am sure you mean kindly," she said gently, "and you may be sure I shall give every consideration to what you have said."

When her strange visitor had gone she sat for a long time quite still in front of her table, staring with unseeing eyes at the many papers scattered upon it. She knitted her black eyebrows and thought and thought, but apparently to no purpose, for presently she said to herself: "What *could* he mean by calling that little boy a misogynist, and what on earth could the child mean about not being a policeman?"

- 61 -

The boy was waiting for the schoolmaster at the gate as he went out. "Well, was it any use?" he cried eagerly.

"My dear chap," said that gentleman, "you are a little noodle. That's what you are."

And the boy, as he trotted by the schoolmaster's side, found something vaguely comforting in this cryptic speech.

PART II
CHILDREN OF LAST CENTURY

A SMALL EVENT

All service ranks the same with God:

If now, as formerly He trod

Paradise, His presence fills

Our earth, each only as God wills

Can work—God's puppets, best and worst,

Are we; there is no last nor first.

Say not "a small event"! Why "small"?

Costs it more pain than this, ye call

A "great event" should come to pass,

Than that? Untwine me from the mass

Of deeds which make up life, one deed

Power shall fall short in or exceed!

Pippa Passes.

Every night the Alfresco Entertainers gave their performance on a little platform set right under the shadow of the great cliff; while in front of them, not a dozen yards away, the rhythmic wash of the sea on a rocky shore seemed a sort of accompaniment to their songs, much softer and more tuneful than that of the poor, jingly, rheumatic piano, which had nothing between it and every sort of weather save an ancient mackintosh cover.

The village itself was but a shelf of shore with one long, straggling, lop-sided street: cottage and shop and great hotel set down haphazard, cheek by jowl, all apparently somewhat inept excrescences on the side of the green-clad cliffs rising behind them straight and steep, a sheer five hundred feet, and just across the narrow line of red road lies the Bristol Channel, with, on a clear day, the Welsh coast plainly in view.

At ten years old, people are generally found more interesting than scenery, and Basil took a great interest in the variety entertainers. They looked so smart and debonair, he thought, in their blue reefers, white duck trousers, and gold-laced yachting caps—though they none of them ever put out to sea. There were five of them altogether, two ladies and three men. Basil did not care so much about the ladies, in spite of the rows of Chinese lanterns that outlined the little stage and shone so pink in the darkness; there seemed no glamor or mystery about them. They were not transcendently beautiful like the gauzy good fairy of pantomime, or the peerless, fearless circus lady in pink and spangles: neither did they possess the mirth-provoking qualities of the dauntless three clad in yatching garb. One always sang sentimentally of "daddies," or "aunties," or "chords," that had somehow gone amissing; and the other—Basil almost disliked that other—sang about things he could in nowise understand, in a hoarse voice, and danced in between the verses, and she didn't dance at all prettily, for she had thick ankles and high shoulders.

But the three "naval gentlemen," as Basil respectfully called them, sang funny songs, and acted and knocked each other about in such fashion as caused him almost to roll off his chair in fits of ecstatic mirth. Nearly every fine night after dinner, if nobody wanted him, Harnet, the tall man-servant, would take Basil, and they sat on two chairs in the front row and listened to the entertainment. Sometimes grandfather himself would come, but he generally went to sleep in his chair at home; for when a man goes peel-fishing all day, walking half a dozen miles up the rocky bank of a Devonshire trout stream to his favorite pool, he is disinclined to move again, once he has changed and dined.

The bulk of the audience attending the Alfresco Entertainment sat on the wall separating shore from road, or on the curbstone, but there were always a few chairs placed directly facing the stage, which were charged for at sixpence each. Harnet was far too grand and dignified to sit on either wall or curbstone, and as grandfather always gave Basil a shilling to put in the cardboard plate, Harnet preferred to spend it in this wise.

Now all that company had high-sounding, aristocratic names, except one, who was called, as Basil said, "just simply Mr. Smith." There was Mr. Montmorency, the manager, whose cheeks were almost as blue as his reefer, and his wife, the lady who danced in the evening, but in the daytime affected flowing tea-gowney garments and large flat hats; there was Mr. Neville Beauchamp, who sang coster songs, to whom the particular accent required for this sort of ditty really seemed no effort, as all his songs were given in similarly pronounced and singular fashion. The lady of the melancholy ballads was called De Vere; she looked thin and young and generally cold, as well she might, for she played everyone's accompaniments, and never wore a coat, however cold the night. But it was for Mr. Smith that Basil felt most enthusiasm. In the first place, his speaking voice was as the voices of "grandfather's friends." In the second, he was, to Basil's thinking, an admirable actor—changing face and voice, even his very body, to suit the part he happened to be playing; and thirdly, he was funny—funny in a way that Basil understood. Even grandfather laughed at Mr. Smith and applauded him, and when the cardboard plate went round, he sent Basil with the first bit of gold they had had that season.

"Clever chap that," he said as they strolled homeward under the quiet stars. "Reminds me of someone somehow—looks like a broken-down gentleman; got nice voice, and nice hands—wonder what he's doing with that lot?"

Basil, however, was quite content to admire Mr. Smith without concerning himself as to his antecedents. He forthwith christened him "the jokey man," and it rather puzzled him that, except at night, the jokey man was hardly ever with the others, but went wandering about by himself in an aimless and somewhat dismal fashion. Could it be that Mr. Montmorency and Mr. Neville Beauchamp were proud, Basil wondered, because they had such fine names.

Basil's face was as round as a full moon, and fresh and fair as a monthly rose. Tall and well set up, he was good at games, and keen on every kind of sport. Long days did he spend up the river with his grandfather fishing for trout— he was to have a license for peel next summer, but had to be content with trout during this. He went sea-fishing, too, in charge of a nice fisherman called Oxenham, and caught big pollock outside the bay, and every morning Oxenham rowed Basil and Harnet out from the shore that they might have their morning swim, for the coast is so rocky and dangerous that bathing from the land is no fun at all—though the rocks are very nice to potter about on at low tide, when energetic persons can find prawns in the pools.

One day as Basil was busily engaged in this pursuit, who should come up behind him but the jokey man, looking as melancholy as though there was no sunshine, or blue water, or pleasant pools full of strange sea beasts. Indeed, although he was by profession such an amusing man, he had by no means a cheerful face. Tired lines were written all round his eyes, his shoulders were bent, and his long slim hands hung loose and listless at his sides, yet it was plain that he was by no means old. Moreover, he had changed his smart yachting suit for an old tweed coat and knickerbockers, and a grey billycock dragged over his eyes bereft his appearance of all traces of the jokey man. So that for a minute or two Basil did not know him, even although he sat down on a rock close by and lit his pipe.

Basil was standing bare-legged and knee-deep in water in pursuit of a particularly active and artful shrimp, so that it was only when he at last lifted his head with an emphatic "bother," that he noticed the stranger; then he beamed, for chance had tossed plump into his lap the opportunity he had long been seeking.

"How do you do?" the little boy inquired politely, taking off his muffin cap with one wet hand while he grasped his net with the other. "I am so pleased to have met you; I've wanted to for ever so long."

"That's very nice of you," said the man, and when he smiled he looked quite young. "I am sure the pleasure is mutual."

"I've something most pertickler to ask you," continued Basil eagerly, scrambling out of the pool to sit on the rock beside him, "and it seemed as if I was never to get a chance. It's not for myself either, it's for Viola—you know Viola by sight, I daresay?"

Now it happened that the jokey man, like most other people in that village, knew Viola by sight very well indeed. In fact, Viola, and the General, and Basil, were as speedily pointed out to every stranger who arrived as though they had been bits of scenery. For they came every summer and the village was proud of them.

"Is she your sister?" asked the jokey man, suddenly taking his pipe out of his mouth.

"Yes, and she's two year older than me, but she doesn't go to school—I've been for a year—she has a ma'mselle. I daresay you've seen us with her. It's been such a bore having her here, but she's going to-morrow, and then we shall do just what we like, for there will be only Harnet and Polly, and we like them. Grannie had to go off quite suddenly to nurse Aunt Alice, and won't be back for a week, so there'll be nobody but grandfather and us; it'll be simply ripping," and Basil paused breathless, beaming at the pleasant picture he had conjured up.

The jokey man put his pipe back into his mouth and waited; but it had gone out, so he just laid it on the rocks beside him, saying:

"What was it you wanted to ask me?"

"It's rather difficult to explain," Basil began, turning very red and rumpling his hair. "It's Viola, you know; she wants so dreadfully to come to your entertainment. I've told her about it, you know, but grandfather says——" Here Basil paused, and turned even redder than before: "One has to be so particular over one's girls, you know," he interpolated apologetically, "and she's the only girl in our family. Grandfather never had any sisters or any daughters, so he thinks no end of Viola, and father and mother are in India, and he says——"

"That some of the songs are vulgar," said the jokey man shortly. "So they are; he's perfectly right."

The jokey man looked at Basil, and Basil looked at the jokey man for a full minute. Then the little boy said very earnestly:

"Do you think that you could persuade them—those other gentlemen, I mean—to leave out one or two songs one evening? There's that one about the 'giddy little girl in the big black hat' that Mr. Montmorency sings. Grandfather doesn't like that one, and it's not very amusing, is it? And Viola *does* want to come so dreadfully."

The jokey man made no reply, but stared straight out to sea with a very grave face. Perhaps he was thinking of all those other Violas who listened night after night to the songs the General objected to, and were perhaps, unlike his Viola, not "cared about, kept out of harm, and schemed for, safe in love as with a charm."

Basil waited politely for some minutes, then, as the jokey man didn't speak, he continued earnestly:

"You see she can just hear that there is music and singing when the windows are open, and it's so tantalizing, and you see it would be rude to walk away when we'd heard you, and come back next time you sang, wouldn't it? It doesn't matter for boys——"

"I'm not at all sure of that," said Mr. Smith hastily; "it matters very much for boys, too, I think—especially if they don't happen to have wise grandfathers with good taste. I'll see what can be done, and let you know."

"Oh, thank you so much!" cried Basil; "that is kind of you. Viola will be so pleased; she's up the village now with Polly, or I'd fetch her to thank you herself."

Now while Basil was talking he noticed that the jokey man's coat had got leather on the shoulders, and that the leather looked as worn as the coat, so he rightly deduced that at some time or another his new friend must have been something of a sportsman, and asked:

"D'you fish at all?"

"Not here," said the jokey man, "but I've done some fishing in my time. Have you had good sport?"

Then immediately ensued a long discussion on the relative merits of flies, and Basil gave forth his opinion, an opinion backed up by the experience of numerous natives, that the "Coachman" was the fly for that neighborhood, but that there were occasions, especially early in July, when exceedingly good results might be obtained by using red ants. They told each other fishing stories. Basil confided to the jokey man that he had just got a beautiful new split cane rod from "Hardy Brothers," promised to show it to him at the earliest possible opportunity, and they speedily became the best of friends. For it is a curious fact that although the actual sport itself is a somewhat taciturn pursuit, there are no more conversational sportsmen in the world than ardent followers of the gentle craft.

Another thing—they are always courteous listeners, and generally full of good stories themselves, yet have the most delicate appreciation of other people's anecdotes. You can nearly always tell a member of a fishing family by this rare and pleasing trait.

Next morning the jokey man called at the hotel and asked for Basil at the door. He wouldn't come in, and when Basil, greatly excited, appeared, only waited to say hastily: "If you like to bring your sister to-night, I think I can promise you that it will be all right." Then fled before Basil could thank him, and was soon pounding up the steep hill that ends abruptly at the hotel door, as though he were training for a mountaineering race.

Basil tore back into their sitting-room to lay the case before his grandfather, who, for once, was lunching in the hotel.

"He promised, you know," he concluded jubilantly, "so she *can* come, can't she?"

Grandfather pulled his moustache and laughed. Then Viola came and laid her fresh soft cheek against his, murmuring pleadingly: "Darling, it would be so lovely," till he pinched Viola's cheek and made stipulations about heavy cloaks, and the children knew the day was won.

And the end of it all was that, at half-past eight that evening, grandfather, Basil and Viola were seated on three chairs in the very middle of the road that ran past the Alfresco Entertainers' stage; but as the road ends abruptly in a precipitous rock some thirty yards further along, there is no fear of being run over by traffic.

What an evening of delight that was! How Basil and Viola laughed, and how pleased was grandfather! Another thing is quite certain—that the Alfresco Entertainers in no way lost by the alterations they had made in their programme; the rest of the audience seemed as pleased as Basil and Viola, and no one appeared to miss the "giddy little girl in the big black hat" the least little bit in the world.

"Really, it's vastly civil of Mr. Thingummy," said grandfather on their way home.

Grandfather and Harnet had gone fishing for the whole day. Mademoiselle had departed, only Polly was left in charge, and she had so bad a headache— she put it down to the close, cloudy weather—that she was fain to go and lie down directly she had waited upon Basil and Viola at their lunch, having given the children permission to go for a walk along the beach.

It was a grey day, humid and still, and, being low tide, there seemed no fresh wind blowing in from the sea as usual. The children scrambled over the rocks, very happy and important at being, for once, left to their own devices, and they decided to make an expedition to a little sandy bay that can be reached from the shore at low tide, and to come back by a steep winding path up the cliffs which terminates in the coach road just above the village.

They had not considered it necessary to confide their intention to Polly, who would certainly have objected. They reached the bay all right, paddled for a little time on the hard, smooth sand, and then set out to climb the path which winds in and out of the side of the cliff for all the world like a spiral staircase up to some nine hundred feet above the sea. This path is so narrow that travelers can only walk in Indian file. On the one side is the steep face of the heather-clad rock, on the other a sheer drop on to the rocks below.

When the children had climbed about a third of the way they found themselves enveloped in white mist—a mist so thick, and fine, and clinging, that you cannot see your own hand held before your face. It was no use to go down again; the tide had turned, and soon the sea would be lapping gently at the foot of the pathway. There was nothing for it but to go on slowly, carefully, step by step, feeling all the time for the rocks on the inner side; by and by the path would widen.

"Don't be frightened, Viola," said Basil cheerfully. "It'll take us a goodish while, but a bit higher up we can walk together."

"I'm not exactly frightened," said Viola in a tremulous voice, "but I rather wish we hadn't come."

"So do I," Basil answered fervently. "If I hadn't been such a juggins I'd have looked up and seen the mist on those cliffs long ago. Probably you can't see that there *are* any cliffs in the village now."

On they toiled, slowly and painfully. It is really a most unpleasant mode of progression, walking sideways up a hill with your back against a very nubbly sort of wall.

"Hark!" cried Basil presently. "Didn't you hear a call?"

The children paused, leant against the cliff, and listened breathlessly. Sure enough someone was calling. It sounded very muffled and far off; but it was plainly a man's voice, and he was calling for help.

"Do you think it's above or below?" Basil asked anxiously. "I can't seem to tell in this fog."

"It must be above, or we should have heard it before. Call out that we're coming."

Basil shouted with all the force of his young lungs, and again the faint, muffled voice answered with a cry for help.

"Come on," exclaimed Basil in great excitement; "we'll find him!" and sure enough in another bend of the path Basil nearly fell over the prostrate figure of a man lying right across it, for here it suddenly grew wider. The man raised himself on his elbow, exclaiming:

"I say, do you think that when you get to the village you could send help? I'm very much afraid that I've broken my leg. I can't stand, and moving at all hurts it no end."

"Why, it's the jokey man!" Basil cried out in dismay. "However did you do it?"

"Oh, dear! oh, dear!" added Viola. "This is sad."

None of them could see the other, but nevertheless, the jokey man knew in a minute who had come to his rescue, and forgot his injuries in his surprise, exclaiming:

"Whatever are you two doing here? Is the General with you?"

"Oh, dear, no," said Viola proudly; "we're *quite* alone, or we shouldn't be here, but isn't it a good thing we *are* here? How did you fall?"

"I was mooning along, not thinking where I was going, when down came the mist. I made a false step and went bang over the edge, but only fell on to the path below, not right over, as I might have done.... Perhaps it would have been better if I had," he added to himself.

"You'd better go and get help, Basil," said Viola decidedly, "and I'll stay and take care of Mr. Smith till they come."

But Mr. Smith wouldn't hear of this. The children helped him to crawl as near the inner side as possible, and when they left him he nearly fainted with the pain of moving. It began to rain, the cold, soft, wetting rain of a Devonshire summer, and Mr. Smith groaned and shivered.

"I am so sorry for you," said a soft voice close beside him. "Is there nothing I could do? Wouldn't you be more comfortable if you were to rest your head in my lap? It would be a sort of pillow. Daddie used to go to sleep like that sometimes out on the moors last summer, when they were home."

"Oh, Viola, Viola!" exclaimed the jokey man, with far more distress than he had yet shown, "why did you stay? You will get cold. It's raining already, and they will be ages."

"There's no use worrying about that," said Viola, edging herself nearer. "We couldn't leave you here all alone and hurt, and Basil wouldn't let me go on to the village 'cause of the fog, so of course I stayed. I hope you won't mind very much; I won't talk if you'd rather not, but I think I'd like to hold your hand if you don't mind. It would be comforting."

The kind little hand was curiously comforting to the jokey man: he insisted on taking off his coat and wrapping Viola in it, in spite of all her protests. Presently the white pall of mist lifted a little and they could see one another, and it certainly was a great pleasure to the man lying against the cliff to watch the little high-bred face with the kind blue eyes turned in such friendly wise toward him. Viola was so like Basil, and yet so entirely individual. Basil's face was round, hers was oval; Basil's nose was broad and indefinite as yet, Viola's nose was small and straight and decided, with the dearest little band of freckles across the bridge. Basil's manner was extremely friendly, Viola's was tender and protecting, and it was such a long time since anyone had taken care of the jokey man, that he almost crooned to himself in the delight of being so tended. She was very tender in her inquiries after his aches and pains, expressed a pious hope that he always wore "something woolly next him," and being reassured on that head, proceeded to suggest that he should smoke if he found it comforting. Then she told him a great deal in very admirative terms about daddy, and grandfather, and Basil, for Viola was of that old-fashioned portion of femininity that looks upon her own mankind as beings of stupendous strength and wisdom. The man lay watching her very intently, but it is not certain that he heard half of what she was saying. He had the look of one who was trying to make a difficult decision. The voices of habit and tradition called very loudly to him just then—dared he listen?

Presently Viola's voice ceased. She was evidently waiting for an answer, and none came.

"Have you any sisters, Mr. Smith?" she repeated.

Mr. Smith shook his head, then he raised himself on his elbow, saying earnestly:

"Look here, Viola! I want you to tell me exactly what you think about something. Suppose Basil—of course it's utterly impossible, but still— suppose that when he was grown up he did something that annoyed you all very much, something disappointing and entirely against his father's wishes"—he paused, for Viola looked very grave and pained—"and then," he continued, "if he went right out of sight, and you, none of you, heard anything more about him for nearly a year—supposing *then* he was sorry, said he was sorry——"

"We should never lose sight of Basil," said Viola decidedly, her eyes dark and tragic at the mere thought. "At least, I'm sure I shouldn't; whatever he did I should love him just the same. You don't love people for their goodness— you love them because they're *they*."

"Are you sure?" asked the jokey man earnestly.

Viola looked hard at him, turned very red, and said shyly:

"Do you think you could tell me just what you did? I know it's you."

The man leant back against the wall again.

"It's not an interesting story," he said wearily, "but it may pass the time. I was at the 'varsity, Cambridge. I was always very fond of acting, and I was extravagant and lazy, too. The very term I went in for my degree I was acting in the A.D.C., and—I was plucked. My father was furious. Then came a whole sheaf of debts. He said I must go back to a small college, live on next to nothing, work, and take my degree. Instead of taking my punishment like a man, I quarreled with everybody, vowed I'd go on to the stage, and came to this. I have kept body and soul together, and I don't think I've done anything to be ashamed of since, but I'm sick and sorry at the whole business. Yet now that I'm all smashed up and useless, it seems somehow mean to go back. My father's a parson, you know, not over well off, and there are a good many of us."

All the pauses in his story, and there were a good many, had been punctuated by Viola with reassuring little pats, and now that the pause was so long that he seemed to have finished his story, she turned a beaming face toward him.

"How *glad* they will be!" she exclaimed. "You must write to-night directly you get back. How *glad* your mother will be!"

A spasm of pain crossed his face. "My mother died just before I left school," he said.

Viola's eyes filled with tears, and she had just exclaimed, "And you have no sisters either, you poor dear?" when the rescue party, accompanied by Basil and the nearly frantic Polly, appeared just below them. They carried the jokey man to the foot of the cliff and took him back to the village in a boat, and as his ankle proved to be very badly broken he elected to go into the cottage hospital on the hill. The long wait in the wet, that had not in the least hurt Viola, proved altogether too much for the jokey man. That night he became feverish and delirious, and when the children and the General went to ask for him next day, they were told that he was very ill indeed, and that the broken ankle was quite a small matter in comparison with the pneumonia. That evening the doctor called on the General, and directly the performance was over, the General went to see the Alfresco Players at their lodgings.

"Do you happen to know who his people are?" the General asked Mrs. Montmorency.

"He never let on that he'd got any folks, poor fellah," she answered with a sob. She had a kind heart if her ankles were thick. "He was never one to talk about himself, and he's never had so much as a postcard by post since he's been here, that I do know. His real name's not Smith at all; all his linen—beautiful and fine his shirts are too—is all marked 'Selsley.'"

"Have you no idea what part of the country he came from?" the General asked. "Then we could look in a directory. It would be a horrible thing if——"

"He joined us in London," Mrs. Montmorency gasped between her sobs, while her tears made little pathways on her painted cheeks. "He hadn't any references, but I persuaded my husband to take him. He carried his references in his face, I said, and so I'm sure we've found it, for a nicer, more obliging, gentlemanly——"

"Do you think, sir," Mr. Montmorency interrupted, "that he told the little lady anything about himself when they were up on the cliff together?"

"God bless my soul!" exclaimed the General in great excitement. "Of course he did; I have it. Who has got a clergy list?"

Naturally none of the Alfresco Players possessed such a work, and it was already too late to knock up the vicar of the parish. But next morning the General called on the vicar very early, and then despatched an exceedingly long telegram to the post office and several bottles of champagne to the cottage hospital, where Polly, Basil and Viola hung about the doors all the morning hoping for better news. The Alfresco Players got out a green leaflet to the effect that there would be that night a benefit performance for that talented artist, Mr. Smith, who had been suddenly stricken down by serious illness. The General seemed to send and receive a great many telegrams, and did not go fishing all that day. At sundown there was no better news at the hospital, and it seemed exceedingly probable that the jokey man would joke no more. The General met the last train, and drove away from the station accompanied by an elderly, severe-looking clergyman. They stopped at the hospital and the clergyman went in.

The jokey man was so noisy and talked so continuously that the hospital authorities had him moved from the men's surgical ward into a little room by himself. As the matron showed the strange clergyman into this room, a nurse rose from the chair at the bedside. The jokey man's voice was no longer loud, but he kept saying the same thing over and over again.

"All day long he keeps repeating it," she whispered. "I'm so thankful you've come, for he can't possibly last if this restlessness continues."

"I'm sure he'll come if you send," the weak, irritable voice went on. "Why don't you send? I want my father—'father, I have sinned'—that's it—'father, I have sinned'—but I know he'll come if you send. I want my father, I tell you—why won't you send? I want my father."

The whispering voice persisted in its plaint, the hot hands plucked at the sheet when other hands closed over them, holding them firmly, and the voice he was waiting for said quietly:

"My dear son, I am here."

As the sick man raised his tired eyes to the grave grey face bent over him, his troubled mind was flooded with an immense content, his poignant restlessness was calmed.

"Good old father!" he said softly, and lay quite still.

The jokey man thought better of it, and didn't die after all. In another week Basil and Viola were allowed to go and see him. They stood very hushed and solemn on either side of his bed, for he looked very thin and white, and was still lying right on his back, which made him seem more ill somehow. For quite a minute nobody said anything at all, till Basil, who held a large folded bracken leaf in his hand, laid it down on the jokey man's chest and spread it out. A fish speckled with brown reposed in solemn glory in the midst.

"It's for your dinner," whispered Basil. "It's only four ounces off the pound. I caught it myself two hours ago. Viola saw me do it. I think a 'Coachman's' the best fly after all."

IN DURANCE VILE

Gabrielle always remembered the day that the ringmaster of the circus came to see her pony jump. She was proud of her pony, who was dapple grey and Welsh, and could jump nine inches higher than himself.

Gabrielle was five, and had ridden without a leading rein for two years, but her father never let her jump Roland, the pony. So the pony jumped by himself, greatly to the edification of the ringmaster who had been bidden to see the feat.

While all this was going on, Nana called her to nursery tea, and as she trotted down the long yard, past the stables, and towards the drive, the ringmaster turned to Jack Ainslie, Gabrielle's father, and said: "Has the little Missie hurt her foot? She's a thought lame."

Jack Ainslie looked hastily after the idolized little figure, and noted that the ringmaster was right. She *was* a thought lame.

Hastily excusing himself, he ran after the child. "Have you hurt your foot, darling?" he asked anxiously. "You're limping a little. Did you twist your ankle?"

"Oh, no, Daddy dear, I'm not hurt. I'm going to tea." Gabrielle put up her face for the ever-expected kiss and ran after her nurse. Jack Ainslie dismissed the subject from his mind and showed the ringmaster the rest of the horses.

From that day, however, things changed for Gabrielle. Other people noticed the little limp, and her parents, terrified and distressed, sent for the family doctor. He discovered that in some way, probably at birth, her hip had been dislocated, and had formed a new socket for itself, and that henceforth she would limp—unless—and here all the mischief began—something could be done. Her father was frantic. Of course something must be done. That his Gabrielle, his dainty little lady with her pretty face, her quick intelligence, and her gracious ways, should be lame—oh, it was intolerable! He was broken-hearted and rebellious, and even his wife's steadfast patience and unchanging tenderness could not make him resigned. Then began for Gabrielle a series of visits to London. She was taken from one great doctor to another till she grew quite used to marching about on thick piled carpets, clad in nothing but her sunny hair, while they discussed her interesting "case."

"Doctors are chilly men," said Gabrielle; "their hands are always cold to my body."

An operation was arranged, but at the last moment Jack Ainslie drew back, for the surgeons would not guarantee success, and the family doctor said grave things about Gabrielle's constitutional delicacy. So it was decided that more gradual means must be tried to bring about the desired result. The "gradual means" assumed the shape of an instrument, hideous to behold and painful to wear. It broke Jack Ainslie's heart to see his little lady cabined and confined in such a cruel cage, and for the little lady herself it blotted out the sunshine and made life very grey and terrible. One thing was quite plain to Gabrielle, and that was that evidently Nature was very much to blame in having provided a new "socket" for the poor little dislocated bone. This impertinence must be interfered with at all costs—the doctors seemed to agree upon that. And Gabrielle wondered why it was so wrong to have no pain, to be perfectly unconscious of her "affliction," as her nurse called it, and so interesting (to the doctors) and right, to be uncomfortable and to wear a hideous high-soled boot and an iron cage, with crutches under the arms that pushed her shoulders up to her ears.

As for the instrument, it was designed and ordered by three famous surgeons, and it cost the price of many ponies. Gabrielle tried to be brave. She was curiously conscious that the pain her parents suffered was far greater than her own. The instrument was adjusted in London, and on the way home in the train her mother asked her many times, "Does it hurt you, my darling?" And Gabrielle always answered bravely, "I can bear it, mother dear; I can bear it!"

When she got home that night, the poor little leg was black from the cruel pressure, and Mary Ainslie broke down and cried till she could cry no longer. Gabrielle tried to walk bravely in her cramping irons, and to smile at her parents when she met their troubled eyes. At first she broke the thing continually, for she was an active child, much given to jumping off chairs and playing at circus on the big old sofa. But by and by all desire to jump and run left her. She grew high-shouldered, and would sit very still for hours, while her daddy told her stories or drove her behind Roland in a little basket-carriage he had bought for her. Truly the iron entered into her soul, the cruel iron that cramped the child's soft body; and Gabrielle's eyes grew larger and larger, and her chin more pointed, while the once plump little hands were white as the petals of the pear-blossom outside the nursery window.

"I wish people wouldn't ask me about it; they are kind, but I wish they wouldn't," Gabrielle would say. "I'm tired of telling them about the socket, and I'm not 'a poor little soul'—I'm daddy's little lady!"

There came to Jack Ainslie a very old college friend, a doctor, Gabrielle's godfather, and devoted to her, and he was supremely dissatisfied with her treatment and implored them to take her to see a young surgeon, a friend of his own, who was making a great name, and doing wonders for everyone who came under his care. Jack Ainslie and his wife needed but small persuasion, and it was decided that Gabrielle should go to London as soon as possible.

What hastened the visit was this: Gabrielle was devoted to fairy lore, and a favorite play of hers was to be the beautiful princess who is freed from giants and dragons and lions by the gallant "Boots" of the Norse tales. Her father always enacted the part of that redoubtable third son, and was wont to kneel before her, making extravagant protestations of his devotion, which she accepted with gracious condescension. On this particular afternoon, just after tea, her father proposed to play the favorite game, but Gabrielle would have none of it. "I can't be a princess any more, Daddy; I'm sure no princess ever wore an instrument!" she said. "I don't feel like a princess any more at all." Her father caught her up in his arms, with a great hard sob, which frightened her, and she stroked his face, saying tenderly: "Don't be sorry, dear, dear Dad! I didn't mean to hurt you. I'll be a princess, I will, indeed! I *will* feel like a princess really!" The next day Jack Ainslie and his wife took Gabrielle up to town. They did not even take the faithful Nana, for Gabrielle's mother could hardly bear to let any hands but hers touch her darling, ever since the day that the ringmaster had made his sad discovery.

Mary Ainslie took Gabrielle to the new doctor the following morning, while Jack sat in the smoking-room of the hotel, lighting innumerable cigars which he did not smoke, and turning over illustrated papers which he did not see. Then he turned out of the hotel and walked down Piccadilly, blundering into the passers-by, and when he crossed the road, was nearly ridden over by an omnibus, so blind and stupid was he in his heavy sorrow. Poor Jack! his honest heart was very full of grief, for he loved his little lady dearly, and he felt that unless something were done quickly, he would soon have nothing but a tender memory to love.

Gabrielle and her mother were shown into the new doctor's consulting-room at once. He was a tall young man, with red hair and keen green eyes. Her mother undressed Gabrielle, all but the "instrument," which clasped the tender little body, and seemed so cruelly unnecessary. The young doctor frowned when he saw it, then he took it off himself, and Gabrielle noticed that his touch was as gentle as her mother's, and that his hands were warm. She gave a happy little shake when she was free of it, a little wriggle and jump of relief. Then the doctor made her walk, and felt her all over, after which he rolled her up in a big fur rug, to sit in front of the fire, while he went into the next room with her mother. They were not long away, and on their return Gabrielle looked up at the doctor with bright, curious eyes.

"Does the instrument hurt you?" he asked. Gabrielle looked at it, as it leaned feebly against a chair, and said: "It does, rather; but it does its best not to. I think...!"

"Well, any way, you're not going to wear it any more. Are you glad?"

"But what will the socket do?"

"Bless me, child; they've talked about you far too much. The socket will do beautifully—much better without it than with it!"

"May I wear shoes like other little girls?"

"Certainly; the prettiest shoes that can be got!"

"Not compensatum shoes?"

"No; ordinary shoes, exactly alike!"

By this time Gabrielle had been arrayed in some clothes. She noticed that her mother's hands trembled, but that her eyes were glad. The child looked up at the tall young doctor, who was watching her with his keen green eyes, and said: "My Daddy will be so glad. He will look at me, and not look so sorry, and there will be no hard things to stick into him when he cuddles me! He will be so glad!"

The doctor made a queer little sound in his throat; then he lifted Gabrielle in his arms and carried her to the window.

"Do you see the end of this street," he asked, "where the roar and the rumbling sound comes from? That's Oxford Street. Well, in that street is a beautiful shop full of shoes—shoes for little girls—and you are going there directly, to get the prettiest pair that mother can find for you!"

"May they have silver buckles?" Gabrielle asked eagerly.

"I think it extremely advisable they should have big silver buckles. You will walk both fast and far in buckles shoes, and you must learn to dance the *tarantella*, and all the dolls will sit in a row to watch you!"

Gabrielle gave a delighted laugh. "Will the leg that wore the irons get fat again, like the other?"

"Oh, dear, yes! You mustn't think about that leg any more, but you must do all the exercises mother is going to show you, and when you can hang on a trapeze for twenty minutes, without falling off, you must write and tell me."

Then Gabrielle's mother finished dressing her, all but her boots. The boot with the "compensatum" sole lay near the instrument. Gabrielle looked at it with great aversion. "It's a very dry day," said she. "May I go to the cab in my stockings, and not put on no shoes till I have my new ones?"

The doctor pushed the little boot out of sight, under the chair, with his foot, and said: "I'll carry you to the cab, and mother or the cabman will carry you to the shop across the pavement, and you shall never see that iron horror or that boot again!"

As the doctor carried her across the hall, Gabrielle put her arms round his neck, and kissed him on both his eyes.

"Your eyes taste very salt!" she said, "But you are the best doctor in the world!"

THE SURRENDER OF LADY GRIZELL

Geordie had found the world a rather draughty place since that March morning when his mother went out hunting and was brought back in a strange secret fashion, and he saw her face no more.

"Your poor Ma's met with a haccident, Master Geordie—poor lady she've broke her back and now she's gone to 'Eaven."

So Nana explained things to him. New black clothes came from the tailor's, and Geordie went with Nana to lay flowers upon his mother's grave.

At five years old discomfort is felt, rather than defined; Geordie was conscious of a difference, an uncomfortable difference in his surroundings, but by no means directly traced its cause to the loss of his mother. Nor was he actively miserable. It is true that he sometimes wondered why Nana so often omitted his bath in the morning, and why he was never dressed to go down in the evening; but in some respects he had quite a dissipated time. So many people asked him out to tea, and amusement of which Nana distinctly approved, for she went too.

Geordie regarded his father with immense admiration, he was so tall, and handsome, and jolly. But since that day when everything was altered, the Hon. Donald Cochran found less time than ever to devote to Geordie. It is true he did not go out hunting any more, but he seemed always to be shut up in that hitherto almost unused room—called the "study," sorting papers and interviewing stout gentlemen, who wore aggressive watch-chains, and whose footsteps were much lighter than those of the hunting friends who used to come about the house.

After a month of vague loneliness and discomfort there came a change in Geordie's fortunes. His aunt, Lady Grizell Fane, who had been abroad at the time of Mrs. Cochran's death, appeared upon the scene.

A tall woman, with keen grey eyes, a woman who observed much and said little—Lady Grizell after three days realized the exact position of affairs. On the fourth day she went back to the Towers, taking Geordie with her.

Lady Grizell was one of those women, so often childless, in whom the maternal instinct is passionately alive. The love of children was a religion with her, and all the love she would have lavished on her own child had the fates bestowed one on her, she lavished upon Geordie.

The world suddenly became a sunny, sheltered place for the lonely little boy. Baths were plentiful and nursery tablecloths were clean, as meals were regular. Above all, somebody wanted him, somebody took an interest in his doings, and a great warm human love "enwheeled him round." A new experience this for Geordie—no one had ever been actively unkind to him, his mother had looked after his creature comforts thoroughly. He was always well dressed and well tended, but she had never found his society particularly interesting, nor did she manifest any desire to see him often during the day. Though a fine strong child, he was too like the Cochrans to be pretty. Big nose, grey eyes, thin face, high cheekbones, and dogged mouth, may be well enough in a man, but in a child are apt to be all indefinite and out of proportion. No, Geordie was not a pretty child. Neither was he very clever; but he was honest and kind-hearted, and he worshipped those who were kind to him, Aunt Grizell most of all.

Uncle Fane was a philanthropist, absorbed in blue books and statistics. When Parliament was sitting he went to London, while Aunt Grizell not infrequently preferred to remain with Geordie at the Towers.

Geordie learned to ride with his aunt (his father had never been able to afford a pony for him, it takes such a lot of money to keep hunters), he did gardening with her, and with her he learned to read indifferently well. But he learned many things more important than these.

He learned to be immensely proud of "the family," to hold the reigning house in due respect certainly, but with reservations in favor of one Charles Edward, and his descendants, for whose sake "the family" had greatly dared and suffered. He learned that he must be courteous and deferent in his manners, true and just in all his dealings, and that he must control his temper, which, like that of the rest of the family, was inclined to be hasty. Moreover, he quickly discovered that his aunt *was* herself all she would have him be. To know that a thing grieved her was enough with Geordie to prevent its happening again, so they were very happy.

His father came from time to time to spend a few days at the Towers, praised his improved appearance, and his seat in the saddle, took him out shooting on occasions, and was always profuse in his thanks to his sister for her care of the boy.

But this happy and peaceful state of things was not to last. A cloud came over the horizon. Lady Grizell went about with red eyes and a harrassed look, and Geordie found Uncle Fane regarding him with an expression, kindlier than of yore certainly, but in which he discovered so large a proportion of pity that he resented it, without knowing why.

Then Lord Lochmaben, his father's eldest brother, came to the Towers. During his visit, the child was always hearing scraps of conversation in which the words "madness," "that woman," and "social suicide" occurred with bewildering frequency. He felt that in some mysterious way these irrelevant remarks had some bearing on his own fortunes. Lord Lochmaben also regarded him with that strange pitying expression, and during his lordship's visit, Aunt Grizell's eyes were redder, and her manner more perturbed than ever.

At last, one morning at the end of May—Geordie will always hate the scent of the lilacs—Lady Grizell called him from his play to come to her in the morning room.

He came, running through the open French window, and when he reached his aunt's chair she put her arm round him, saying huskily: "Geordie dear! your father wants you at home, until September—and then you are to go to school!"

Lady Grizell made the announcement abruptly. To her surprise it was received in absolute silence. Geordie was, as his aunt herself would have said, "utterly dumbfoundered." To go to school some day was natural and proper—but to go home.... "Why does father want me now?" asked Geordie in a shaky voice. The Hon. Donald never betrayed any distress at parting from him when he left the Towers—what could it mean?

The child was very like "the family," he was not at all demonstrative, and he "thought shame" to cry.

He flung his arms round his aunt, holding her so tight that the buttons of his Norfolk jacket made deep dents on her cheek, and Lady Grizell could hear how painfully the little heart was thumping.

There was silence for a minute between these two who understood each other so well; then Geordie asked: "When am I to go, Aunt Grizy?"

"In a week—oh, what shall I do without you, my bonnie man?"

"But I shall come to see you often, shan't I? Papa won't want me all the time, and you will ask him to let me come often, won't you, Aunty?"

Lady Grizell stroked his hair tenderly, but she could not deceive even a child, and she shook her head.

"I'll ask him, my dear, you may be sure. But I fear he may not be able to grant my request. Unfortunately, there is a subject upon which your father and I cannot agree, and he is vexed with me, and naturally wants his son for himself."

"Is it that 'suicide woman' that is the subject?" asked Geordie breathlessly.

Lady Grizell gazed at him in thunderstruck amazement. "What *do* you mean, child?"

"Well, whenever I was out walking with Uncle Lochmaben and Uncle Fane, I kept hearing little bits about 'that woman' and 'suicide' and papa, so I thought it might be that. I didn't listen, truly—I couldn't help hearing, and I didn't understand."

Lady Grizell put back the hair from the boy's square forehead and looked into his honest grey eyes, then she spoke:

"Geordie dear, there are always things in life that we cannot understand, and things we cannot help; what we must do is to be as brave and honest as we can, and leave the rest to God. Your dear father is very lonely and he has recently married a lady who will be your new mamma. You must try to be as good and courteous and obedient to her as you are to me—and Geordie, son! don't forget me!"

Here Lady Grizell broke down, and Geordie thought it no shame to cry too.

That week was terribly short. At the end of it Geordie went out into the draughty world again, while Lady Grizell went about saying like her more famous namesake: "Oh, werena my heart lecht I wad dee!"

Geordie could never be induced to speak much about the three months that followed. During those three months Lady Grizell grew thin and pale.

One morning she received a letter from the Hon. Donald in which he informed her that he and his wife had made arrangements for Geordie to go in September to an excellent school in the Forest of Dean where boys received board and education for the modest sum of twenty guineas a year.

Lady Grizell gave a little cry, and stared at the letter in her hand as though it had been some horrible phantom. Then she flew downstairs and into her husband's study, where he sat writing a report for the Society of Agriculture.

"Augustus, read this! I am going to see Donald to-day, and tell him that I will receive his wife—I can't let my pride stand in the way of that child any longer—read this!" and she thrust the letter under her husband's aristocratic nose.

Mr. Fane put on his glasses, read the letter, took them off, folded them up and put them in the case—a methodical, deliberate man, Mr. Fane—then he said slowly:

"Have you considered what people will say? Have you forgotten that everybody knows her most unpleasant story?"

"I cannot help it. People must say what they please. I will not have Geordie go to such a school, even if I have to receive half the fallen women in London to prevent it. If Lochmaben never marries, Geordie will be head of our house."

Lady Grizell spoke with passionate excitement. Mr. Fane felt that he hardly knew his wife, always so gentle and dignified, in this woman with the pale face and blazing eyes. He expostulated forcibly and at his usual length. If he was somewhat less conscious of the dignity of the House of Cochran than was Lady Grizell, he was keenly alive to the dignity of the House of Fane. But all his exhortation, all his arguments were of no avail. He could not shake Lady Grizell's determination; and the afternoon saw her speeding in the express toward the interview with her brother.

The journey was not long, but the August day was hot. Lady Grizell felt faint and shaken when the omnibus (she had been too excited to wire for a cab) deposited her at her brother's door.

The parlormaid looked curiously at the tall lady who asked so pointedly for *Mr.* Cochran, and showed her into the study. No ladies ever called, and here was an undoubted lady—"my lady" to boot—as the sharp girl discovered on reading the card.

She carried the card to her master in the garden, where he was sitting with his wife. He flushed as he read it, and tossed it to the woman beside him, exclaiming: "Grizie, by Jove!—can she be coming round?"

The woman caught the card, reading the name aloud in an eager, excited voice, then said, a little bitterly: "She only asks for *you*."

"She wouldn't come here to insult you. I know Grizie. It's something about the boy, and she wants to be friends. You wait here till I send for you."

He strode across the lawn, and entered the study by the open French window.

"Now this is really good of you, Grizie; Geordie will be in raptures—it's kind and friendly!"

Lady Grizell was pale, and the cheek she turned to his kiss was very cold. She clasped her hands to stay their trembling and began in a low voice:

"Donald! you said that if I would receive Mrs. Cochran——"

"Nelly, you mean!" interrupted the Hon. Donald.

"If I would receive your wife—you would let me keep Geordie. If I promise to ask you both to the Towers—twice every year—will you let me have him, instead of sending him to that horrible school—will you, Donald? I'll educate him, he shall cost you nothing—I have a little money, you know, and Augustus is very generous to me—will you let him come to me?"

Donald looked rather shamefaced as he muttered: "Isn't it rather like selling the little chap?"

"But it's selling him into happiness, Donald: he is such a dear lad, and he loves me, and ... it isn't very easy for me!"

There was silence for two minutes. Lady Grizell's heart thumped in her ears.

Overhead there was a sudden patter of little feet, and Lady Grizell sank upon her knees, sobbing: "Oh, give him to me, Donald, for God's sake, give him to me! I cannot bear it!"

Donald's eyes were red as he raised his sister and gently put her in an easy chair. He patted her shoulder soothingly, and his voice trembled as he said: "Look here, Grizie! you shall have the boy. There shall be no bargain between us; I never meant to send him to that beastly school. I tried it on to fetch you—as it has—but I can't play the game so low down as that—I don't set up for a model parent. I know you'll bring him up better than we should. You can leave this house without meeting my wife if you prefer it, and I'll send Geordie to you to-morrow. But, if you like to do a kind and generous thing to a woman who has known little but unkindness, and shame, and sorrow all her life, and who is a good and loyal wife to me, then I say, God bless you, Grizell Cochran, for you are a good woman!"

Donald was not given to the making of long speeches. His voice broke many times in the course of this, and the tears were running down Lady Grizell's pale cheeks. She held out her hands to him, saying simply, "Take me to her!" and the two tall figures went out across the grass together.

A CLEAN PACK

Basil sat alone in the schoolroom, although it was past bedtime. Nurse, like everybody else, had apparently forgotten him, but Basil, absorbed in his own thoughts, sat on by the dying fire. There were always fires in his grandfather's house whenever it was in the least cold, and that August it was very cold, so cold that grandfather, getting wet through out shooting, somehow got a chill, was ill only three days, and now was lying dead in the big bedroom over Basil's head. So Basil had a good deal to think about. It was not that death was new to him—from his earliest infancy it had been impressed upon him that his father was dead—but that he could not by any stretch of fancy imagine what life would be without grandfather—grandfather who was lying with his beautiful hands crossed on his breast in that long, light-colored wooden box upstairs.

Basil resented the fact that grandfather's coffin should be made of light wood. It seemed incongruous and impertinent, somehow, that anything used by grandfather should be otherwise than old—old and rich-colored and seemly; and the child found himself wondering whether grandfather was annoyed. There were many things in that bedroom calculated to annoy him, Basil reflected. In the first place, when mother took him in that afternoon that he might lay the asters gathered in his own garden at his grandfather's feet, he remarked that all the blinds were down, and grandfather would have hated that, and the windows were shut, and there was a heavy scent of hot-house flowers. "I fear he's very uncomfortable," whispered Basil to himself. "He'll be glad to get to heaven out of that stuffy room." For grandfather had loved air as much as he liked fires.

The horizon of Basil's experience was somewhat limited. It consisted of mother and grandfather, and of "other grandfather," who lived at Altringham in Cheshire, and was mother's father.

Every year Basil and mother went to Altringham for six weeks, and life there was so utterly different from what it was with grandfather that Basil never ceased to puzzle over it and to wonder why mother always cried when she came away, and why "other grandfather" always said: "You moost bear with the old heathen, Sophia; he's been generous enough as regards mooney, and, remember, you can be *in* the world but not of it."

There were aunts, too, at Altringham, who made a great fuss of Basil for about three days, and then seemed to find him greatly in the way; while "other grandfather" had a most embarrassing way of suddenly demanding: "Well, yoong mon, and how's the ciphering?"

Basil loved his mother very dearly, but he could have wished that she took life a little less sadly. A gentle melancholy characterized her every thought, and the child felt rather than understood that her mental attitude toward her father-in-law was that of a deprecating disapproval. Grandfather felt it too, for only a week before Basil had heard him say to one of the gentlemen who were tramping the stubble with him: "We shall never understand each other, my poor little daughter and I, though we've lived together seven years. She's as good as gold, and I don't think I'm particularly *difficile*, but there it is—we can never get the same focus for anything." Basil was walking just behind with the keeper, who blushed up to the roots of his hair as he called out: "I'm here, you know, grandfather."

Grandfather pulled up short and turned to look at Basil. Then he gave a queer little laugh. "There's not much Manchester about the boy," he said, and tramped on.

They all went to London from November till the end of March, and there grandfather generally dined at his club and played whist afterward, while Basil's mother had supper with him or had friends of her own to dinner, just as she liked. Grandfather could not get on without his rubber. Even in the country, three times a week three broughams drove solemnly up the drive, and three old gentlemen descended therefrom to dine with grandfather and play whist afterwards.

In London on fine nights he walked to his club, and Basil used to watch him go from the nursery window just as he was going to bed; and at the lamp grandfather always stopped and looked up at the curly head pressed against the pane, then he would lift his hat with a grand sweep and walk on, while Basil hugged himself with the delighted conviction that *his* grandfather was the very handsomest old gentleman in the whole world. And sometimes grandfather would crush his hat over his eyes, while a spasm of pain crossed his clean-shaven, stately old face, and he'd whisper to himself: "My God! how like he is to my poor boy."

Among the very first things that Basil ever learned were the different "suits" in cards. Grandfather taught him and gave him a shilling for every suit as he knew them and the values of the cards, as in whist. Then he taught Basil whist, playing double-dummy, and explaining as they went along: "I wish you, Basil, to play whist as a gentleman should, carefully and with due consideration, with the intelligence and respect that the game deserves, not like a counter jumper for penny points."

It must be confessed that Basil took to this instruction much more kindly than to that included under the heading of "ciphering," or even of reading and spelling. At six he could play a "fair hand," at which he was somewhat puffed up, the only drawback being that mother did not seem to take any interest in his achievements. She never played herself, though grandfather impressed upon her that she was preparing for herself an unhappy old age; in fact, she did not seem to like cards at all.

One very wet Sunday grandfather had arranged four "hands" on the library table, and was proceeding to play a game out of "Cavendish" for Basil's instruction, when his mother suddenly came into the room. She gave one quick glance at the table with the cards, and came forward and stood beside it, saying very quietly: "I do not wish Basil to play cards on Sunday."

Grandfather had risen to his feet as Basil's mother entered the room. It would never have occurred to him to sit down while his daughter-in-law was standing; he swept the cards into a little heap with one swift movement of his beautiful white old hands, and said, with a grave little bow:

"I apologize, my dear. I had for the moment forgotten your—er—convictions on this question. What *may* we play at?—for I've made a bet with myself to keep Basil amused till teatime, and I don't want to lose it." Then, turning to Basil—who, conscious of the thunder in the air, felt very unhappy indeed: "It's not your fault, my boy. You've not been naughty. It's I who was forgetful."

Basil's mother looked from one to the other a little piteously. She had no weapons wherewith to meet her father-in-law's smiling courtesy. She might have liked him better had he sometimes been rude. "Other grandfather" was not uniformly courteous.

On Sunday mornings they all three went to church together, and grandfather sat under the big carved tablet which set forth how Basil's father had died at Ulundi, "aged twenty-nine." Grandfather always carried his daughter-in-law's prayer book for her up to the house, discussed the sermon with her, and was, as he himself would have put it, "vastly agreeable."

A piece of coal fell out on the hearth and startled Basil out of his reverie. He had evidently come to some decision, for he nodded his head emphatically, muttering: "I'd better do it. I'm sure he'll be bored if I don't, and I mayn't get another chance."

The room was quite dark but for the flickering firelight, which had brightened since that big piece of coal fell apart. Basil went to his own special cupboard and took from it a pack of cards, which his grandfather had given him only last week. Grandfather never used the same pack on two consecutive evenings, and gave one to Basil nearly every week with the instruction: "Never use dirty cards, even to build castles with." The child had never played with the ones he held in his hands, and his big grey eyes filled with tears as he wrapped them up in a leaf torn out of his copy-book. Then, laboriously, for Basil was no scribe, he wrote on the packet, a proceeding which took a considerable time. He gave a sob as he kissed his message, but there was no time to be lost. Slipping off his shoes, he opened the door very softly, raced across the hall and up the stairs. The staircase was quite dark, for Chapman had forgotten to light the lamps.

When he reached his grandfather's bedroom door he paused with his hand on the handle. His heart was pounding in his ears, and for a full minute he could not hear whether all was quiet in the room or not. Opening the door very softly, and as softly shutting it after him, he ran across the room and pulled up the blind of the big window that faced the bed. The moon came out from behind a bank of cloud, as if to aid him in his task, and shone full on that strange last couch at the foot of the bed in which grandfather lay so still under his coverlet of flowers. Basil pushed at the heavy window, but it was fastened far out of his reach, and he could not let in the fresh night air that grandfather loved. As his eyes grew accustomed to the lighter room, he came and stood by that light-colored box that he hated so, lifted the white cloth covering his grandfather's face, and looked at him long and earnestly.

Basil had very vague notions as to what heaven was like; but, on reviewing all that he had heard of it, he came to the conclusion that if there was no whist there grandfather would be dull, and he had often heard him say: "There's only one thing that I dread, and that's boredom." So Basil had decided that at all costs such a contingency must be avoided, and grandfather must teach the angels to play whist. "They can p'obably make more cards when they've seen them," said Basil to himself, and pushed his little packet underneath the folded hands, kissed them, and turned to go as softly as he had come.

But the door opened at that moment, and his mother, candle in hand, stood on the threshold gazing at the little figure standing full in the strand of moonlight thrown across the carpet.

"What are you doing here, Basil?" she asked breathlessly.

"I came to give something to grandfather. Oh, don't take it away from him!"

The passionate distress in the child's voice moved her.

"I will take nothing away from him that you wish to give him. But what is it? Is it flowers?"

"No, mother, it is not flowers."

She came into the room, closing the door after her.

"I must see what it is," she said very gently.

Basil stood where he was as though turned to stone. Would she take it away—or would she put it back? He could not see her, for he stood with his back to her, and seemed incapable of turning round. His mother, noting the disarrangement of the flowers, drew out the little packet, and, holding her candle close, read the inscription in the large uncertain writing:

"DEAR GRANDFATHER,

"I'm sory it's not a cleane pak, but I don't know where they are.

"Your loving boy,
"BASIL."

AN IRON SEAT

He sat at one end of the seat, she at the other, and the seat was on the cliffs overlooking the sea at Wolsuth on the Suffolk coast. They say that if your eyes were strong enough you could see the coast of Holland; but even with telescopes no one has yet succeeded in doing that.

At first he hardly noticed her—she was so small and still and read her book so assiduously; but she could have passed a searching examination as to his appearance, for she had studied it carefully. She would have told you that he was tall, and thin, and dark, and "rather old"; that his beard was grey, though his hair was black and decidedly thin on the top; that his spectacles had gold rims and the eyes behind them were very kind; that his manner struck you as extremely grave and decorous: what impressed her most, however, was that big, dull, paper-covered book he was always reading. She was sure it was dull, for *she* couldn't read a word of it; it was in German—she knew that much, and she had tried to pronounce the title to herself in bed at night, but never came near it at all, for it looked like this: "Mendelejeef Chemie," and it would take a very sharp little girl of ten to make much out of that.

No one ever came to sit between them on that iron seat; it was far from the esplanade, and overlooked a lonely part of the beach where there were no "entertainments." When they had sat there for several days, the man who read "Mendelejeef Chemie" looked up suddenly to find that his companion at the other end of the seat was wiping her eyes with the absurdest little red-bordered handkerchief. She held her book in one hand—a somewhat large and heavy book for such a little hand—and wiped her eyes with the other, and yet the man was sure that she was not unhappy, for her thin brown cheeks were flushed, and though her mouth was tremulous it wore a proud and happy smile. He was devoured by curiosity. What book could it be that had the power to move a little girl in so complex a fashion?

He shifted down the seat toward her; but she was so absorbed in what she was reading that she never looked his way, and he found that the book she held in her hand was "From London to Ladysmith via Pretoria."

Suddenly she looked round and saw him. Quite simply and naturally she offered him a share of her book, saying enthusiastically:

"Isn't it splendid? And my daddie was there through it all."

"Are you ready?" she said presently.

The man nodded, and she turned the page. Then, with tears still shining on her cheeks, she began to read aloud:

"It was a procession of lions. And presently, when the two battalions of Devons met—both full of honors—and old friends breaking from the ranks gripped each other's hands and shouted, everyone was carried away, and I waved my feathered hat and cheered and cheered until I could cheer no longer for joy that I had lived to see the day...."

Here she stopped, and, turning her radiant face to the man beside her, cried:

"Aren't you glad you weren't born in any other century? Isn't it a good thing to be in the world when there are such splendid things happening?"

The man smiled down at her, saying heartily: "It is, indeed!" And straightway they were friends.

Ever afterward they sat in the middle of the seat quite close together, and although Winny—that was her name—continued to read "From London to Ladysmith," she read it aloud, and "Mendelejeef" lay neglected on the far end of the seat.

They talked a great deal about the war, and the man found that this little girl knew all about it, from the battle of Glencoe to the relief of Ladybrand, the name and whereabouts of every regiment, the result of every single engagement big or little.

He learned that last year her father had been home on long leave and had brought them all to Wolsuth, "and oh! we did have a lovely time!" but that this year mother couldn't afford it, "War risks are so expensive, you know," that she—Winny—had been silly enough to get influenza in July, and an aunt had consented to let her come with her own family.

"Mother and the boys—there's three boys younger than me: I'm the eldest— have got to stay at home this year. I'm so sorry, though I'd far rather be with them, only I've *got* to get strong. Daddie said so in his last letter."

The man gathered that her aunt and cousins were not altogether *simpatica*, though Winny never said so; still, every day she came and sat on the iron seat after her bath and talked of her book, for which she had unbounded admiration, and of her own small affairs. Being an excellent listener, the man found himself well amused, for he was one of those people who keep the best part of themselves for old friends and little children, and are always quite misunderstood and unappreciated by casual acquaintances, which lack of appreciation doesn't trouble them in the least.

He learned that one of the "boys" was going into the Royal Engineers, "because there you can live on your pay from the first if you're careful," another into the Artillery, "and we may spare one for the Navy."

"And what are you going to be?" he asked one day, after they had exhaustively discussed the futures of the three boys.

"Oh, I'm going to be a mother," she replied, with immense decision. "You see, you have such a lot of people to take care of you and love you, if you're a mother."

"But you have to take care of them first, haven't you?" he asked.

"Oh, yes, just at first—but afterwards—— You should just see the care we take of mother, daddie and all."

The man looked out to sea and tried to picture the eager little figure at his side as a large comfortable mother of many children. He tried so hard that he forgot to answer her last remark, and she asked anxiously:

"Don't you think it's a good thing to be?"

"Excellent!" he answered heartily. "It is one of the oldest and most honorable professions; mothers are people we can in nowise ever do without."

"That's what I thought," said Winny, in a satisfied voice, "and that's what I'm going to be; I made up my mind years ago."

One day as he arrived at their trysting place he discovered that Winny was crying in right down earnest, and not for joy that Ladysmith had been relieved. The little red-bordered handkerchief was screwed up into a tight, wet ball, and the small figure in blue serge looked very woebegone indeed. She had taken off her fisherman's cowl, and cast it on the ground beside her; and when she saw her friend, instead of waving him a gay welcome as he came up, she shook her curly brown hair round her cheeks to hide her face.

All this was so unlike Winny that the man immediately reflected with dismay that he had not read the morning paper at all carefully. It was possible that some disaster had happened to her father. In those days we were apt to trace all sorrows to South Africa.

"No bad news, I hope?" he said in rather a hesitating way as he came up.

Winny shook her head till her face was entirely hidden by her hair; but she did not answer otherwise.

"You may as well tell me what's the matter," said the man; "it may not be past mending."

Now there was something about this man that inspired confidence; moreover, he offered Winny his own handkerchief, which was large and clean and comforting. So she accepted it, mopped her wet face, shook back her hair, and began: "I don't bathe with the others, you know." Here she paused so long that the man said, "Well?" though it was against his principles to interrupt anybody's narrative.

"I bathe at Herrington's machines," she continued, "where we always bathed last year—daddie too—right far away at the end of the beach. My aunt and cousins bathe where the niggers are, and the concert, and such crowds of people you have to wait ever so long for a machine. So I asked if I might bathe with Herrington like last year, for he's such a nice man, and he takes such care of me, and daddie liked him awfully. There's been Herringtons in Wolsuth since 1400!"

Winny paused after this announcement, evidently expecting comment of some sort.

"That's a long record," said the man, rising to the occasion. "And what was Mr. Herrington before he took to keeping bathing-machines?"

"He was mate on a schooner, and one of his sons is a captain of a merchantman; he's raised himself tremendously. Then there's two sons who help Herrington, and are fishermen in winter; and Mrs. Herrington does washing. Oh, they're such a nice family!" she exclaimed ecstatically.

The man looked out to sea, wondering what on earth all this had to do with her tears. But he was a patient person; so he waited.

"I go home to-morrow," she continued, "and I've had one of Herrington's bathing-machines ever since I came—going on for three weeks now—and he's taken me out in the boat and let me dive and swim, and been so kind and jolly, and to-day, when I asked my aunt for the money to pay him—it's fourpence each time—she wouldn't give it me, and laughed and said that it wouldn't hurt him to take me for nothing this year, he made such a lot out of us last. Think of it!" she exclaimed, clasping and unclasping her hands. "It's his living! It's like taking a leg of mutton from a butcher for nothing. I told auntie that mother would send it to her if she'd let me have it, but she only laughed and said it was nonsense. Of course mother will send it to *him*, but that's not the same. He'll have to think me shabby and ungrateful for nearly three days, for I can't go and say good-bye to him when I've nothing to give him. I've only sixpence. Isn't it dreadful?"

The man reflected that there were people who had no objection to accepting legs of mutton from their butchers, who rather resented the fact that these same butchers ventured on occasion to send in a bill; but evidently the soldier who had been shut up in Ladysmith brought up his children with a different view of their obligations. He was very sorry for Winny, but he didn't dare to offer her the money. There are people to whom one cannot offer money.

"Can't you tell Herrington how you are placed?" he feebly suggested.

"Of course not," the child answered scornfully. "He'd say I was 'more'n welcome' to my baths, and that it didn't matter a pin. It's just because I know he'd gladly give me my baths that it hurts so. It's his *living*," she repeated. As she spoke she stood up and stuffed the little wet handkerchief into her pocket.

The man was sitting with his hands thrust deep into his own, as men will when perplexed or troubled. Winny stood with her back to him, gazing sorrowfully at Herrington's bathing-machines on the distant beach.

The little pocket gaped, and the man succumbed to temptation. Very gingerly he dropped a crown piece into the opening which displayed the drenched handkerchief. Then he stood up. "I'm going by the afternoon train," he said, "so I fear I must say good-bye. But I hope we shall meet again some day."

"I hope so," sighed Winny, as she held up her face to be kissed, and wondered why he seemed in such a hurry and never even asked her to walk back with him.

LÉON

I would have our children taught, so far as teaching can go, to love and admire France, that glorious nation which has done so much and suffered so much for humanity.—WILLIAM ARCHER, 1898.

We did not believe it possible that a boy of nine could wear high-buttoned boots, a pale blue sash, and long hair like a girl's, and yet possess a character unaffected by these deplorable externals. That, in addition to this, he should be French, speaking that "*nimini pimini*" language with perfect ease; and, in further proof of his mental slipperiness, speak English almost equally well— but for a curious roll and rumble of the letter "r" in the back of the throat— was another serious stumbling-block in the way of our liking. It was not natural. Had he been puny, or sallow, or in any way physically "Frenchy" as we supposed it, we should have found him less bewildering. But he was sturdy, ruddy, and fair-haired; tall for his age, and of a frank cheerfulness that was rather engaging. Absolutely unashamed of his inferior nationality, unconscious, seemingly, of those elongated buttoned boots, he would shake back his tawny hair and look you squarely in the face with big blue eyes that smiled. He didn't look a "Molly," somehow, in spite of his hair; but we children were convinced that he "must be one, really," and that what the twins called his "false French smile" was a sort of cloak for the innate cowardice of his disposition.

What induced Aunt Alice to marry a French officer, we could not think! That she and her husband were what mother called "devoted to one another" seemed to us an insufficient explanation. Not only did she marry this foreigner and desert her native land, but she became a Roman Catholic— nurse minded this most and called her a Papist—and she seemed perfectly happy in her exile. She was supposed to be a very beautiful person, but what most impressed us during her rare and brief visits was the quality and quantity of the sweets she brought us; sweets in gorgeous boxes which bore the mystic device *Gouache*. France was, we were convinced, a poor sort of place, but exception must be made in favor of her sweets.

In reflecting upon our general attitude toward France and the French at this time, I am reminded of the man who scornfully held up to ridicule a country so far left to itself as to speak of bread as "Pain."

"But," suggested a more tolerant friend, "we call it bread."

"Ah! it *is* bread, you see."

But to return to Léon. His father's regiment had been ordered to some place in Africa, where they could not take Léon, and as Aunt Alice was going with her husband for at least six months, Léon was sent to us.

Eric and I decided that it was a bore. Jennie, who is queer and contradictory at times, said nothing. She adores Aunt Alice. The twins, who had just been doing the Battle of Waterloo in history, and were rampantly patriotic, expressed grave doubts as to whether it was quite loyal to Queen Victoria to receive Léon at all.

"No one likes to go about all day with a mountebank!" grumbled Eric.

"If only he'd had fewer clothes!" I sighed.

But even the most sanguine destroyer of garments could hardly hope that Léon would wear out the quantity of which he was possessed in less than six months.

The twins and Léon came toward us from the tennis lawn; the twins red and triumphant, Léon red and evidently perturbed. Jennie followed, lingering in the rear; she is lame, not a cripple, you know, but noticeably lame.

"England won!" shouted the twins. They always seemed to speak in a sort of chorus.

Léon sat down on the bank beside us and shook his hair back from his face. He evidently intended to appeal to Eric about something; but just as he opened his mouth to speak, he noticed Jennie.

"Come, my cousin," he called, patting the bank beside him; "we shall have good fortune another time!"

"England won!" chanted the twins again. "We always do!"

"That is not so!" cried Léon angrily. "Why do you speak to despise my country? If you were in France, my guest, we speak not forever of Hastings?"

"Oh, that was ages ago," said Eric judicially; "but you were not fairly matched."

"Léon had me, you see," put in Jennie.

"Not so, my cousin, your play was beautiful," said Léon, and he took her hand and patted it. He had queer affectionate ways, and never seemed to mind showing that he liked people. "We beat them next time."

"I wonder what makes Léon so chummy with Jennie?" I asked Eric half an hour later, as we rested after a hot "single." "Do you think it's because she's the only one of us that couldn't lick him?"

Eric raised himself on his elbows and stared at me.

"Well, of all the chuckle-headed ideas I ever heard! Really, for downright wrong-headedness, give me the average girl. Can't you see, you silly, that it's because she's lame, and the little beggar's sorry for her? He's a good-hearted kid if he is Frenchy, and as to licking, just you wait———"

I felt very much snubbed and rather aggrieved, for only that afternoon Eric had grumbled about Léon's clothes and called him a "mountebank." Boys seem to keep things separate somehow, in a curious way.

One day Jennie and Léon had been sent to the Home Farm to fetch eggs. It was really the twins' turn, but they hid so that they shouldn't have to go, for it was a very hot afternoon. Eric and I went for a stroll through the fields in the same direction to look at a nest of young yellow-hammers in the big paddock. There's a sort of hill in the big paddock, and we saw Jennie and Léon coming down the cart road from the farm; they went by the road because Jennie hates climbing gates—it hurts her. Léon was carrying the eggs and they came very slowly, because Jennie was tired. Toward them came one, Fred Oram, a village boy, not a nice boy at all. He hates us because the head groom gave him a thrashing when he caught him throwing stones at the thoroughbreds.

Fred Oram began to limp like Jennie, and called out:

"'Ullo, Frenchy! Shall I plait your 'air for ya?"

Eric, who happened to be at home because two-thirds of his school got measles and mother was nervous, began to run, and I ran after him; but we were a good way from the gate, and the hedge is too thick to get through. We ran alongside of it, and heard Léon say in his funny, stilted English:

"Please hold the eggs, my cousin!" Then, evidently to Fred: "How dare you to mock at my cousin and insult me?"

As we reached the gate Eric pulled me back.

"Let the kid alone!" he whispered. "He's not afraid."

It reminded me of old King Edward, and "Let the boy win his spurs."

None of the three saw us. Jennie was standing on the grass at the side, looking very red and excited; Fred Oram was pulling Léon's hair and dancing round him, making derisive remarks. Léon wrenched his head away, and with a bound stood in the middle of the road, facing his enemy. In spite of his buttony boots—in spite of his blue sash and his long hair—Fred seemed rather afraid of him, for Léon looked, and was, furious.

For about half a minute they stood looking at each other. Léon shouted, "Lâche! Lâche!"—he forgot to speak English, he was so excited—then, "En garde!"—and there seemed a thousand *r*s in that *garde*—and he sprang on Fred, who went down like a ninepin.

Eric vaulted the gate, yelling excitedly, "By Jove! the kid can box."

Jennie laid down the eggs on the grass, and hid her face in her hands. But she looked through her fingers. I saw her.

In another minute Fred was upon his feet. He was bigger than any of us— even Eric. Léon went at him again, calling out what we supposed to be battle-cries in French, and I do believe that the French alarmed Fred as much as the pommelling. Anyway, down he went again, with Léon on the top of him.

"Time!" shouted Eric, picking upon Léon and wiping his face, which was hard to see, for his nose was bleeding and one eye was swollen.

But Fred got up and began to walk away, remarking with surly dignity:

"I don't care for to fight with no French tiger-cats."

Léon broke away from Eric, and ran after his late foe. Fred stopped and took up a defensive attitude, but Léon went up with his grubby right hand held out.

"Shake!" he cried. "We have foughten; it is over. Shake with me?" And Fred shook. "That was quite English?" asked Léon anxiously, as he came back to be cleaned.

Eric looked at him very kindly. "It was all right," he said; and Léon squared his shoulders with modest pride.

"I never saw such a nose to bleed!" exclaimed Eric, ten minutes later, as the last available handkerchief had been reduced to a crimson, pulpy ball. "There's one sash done for, anyway. I suppose the suit'll wash, which is a pity."

On the way home Eric carried the eggs, and Jennie walked hand in hand with Léon. They rather lagged behind, and presently I heard Jennie whisper—I have very sharp ears:

"Léon, am I so very lame?"

"My little cousin, I do not see you lame at all, except when you are fatigued; and we all of us walk badly when we are fatigued;" and he stopped and kissed Jennie on both cheeks.

I had often heard that the French say what is pleasant at the expense of what is true; but just then I wondered if it was always such a bad thing, for when I turned and looked at my little sister her face was perfectly radiant, and she was hardly limping at all.

"I'll tell you what it is," said Eric, when Léon had been carried off by the authorities to have keys put down his back, his eye bathed, and to be generally cleaned up; and we were all five sitting in solemn conclave on the largest wheelbarrow—the twins had joined us, much excited by recent events—"I'll tell you what it is: you kids must drop that Waterloo business, and we must none of us mind his queer clothes any more. He's a ripping good sort, and, after all, he can't help being French!"

"And he wouldn't help it if he could!" cried Jennie. "France is a great country."

For a wonder nobody contradicted her. We were all busy readjusting preconceived ideas.

THE OLD RELIGION

God is above the sphere of our esteem,

And is the best known, not defining Him.

ROBERT HERRICK.

It's a far cry from a busy street in Leith to a village in the loveliest part of wooded Gloucestershire; but, at eight years old, vicissitude is borne with a calm philosophy seemingly unattainable in later years, and Maggie McClachlan expressed no great wonder at her new environment, rather to the disappointment of her worthy aunt, who was fully aware of her own extreme good nature and condescension in "taking the lassie for the whole summer, and paying her fare *both* ways."

Measles followed by an obstinate "hoast," was the commonplace cause that transported Maggie to this strange new country. The long, roaring, whirring, bewildering journey—in which she was passed by a kindly official into the varied guardianship of such passengers as were going her way—left her dazed and puzzled, but not unhappy. Her childless uncle and aunt were kind, and there were the woods.

The first thing that struck Maggie about these woods was the singular absence of bits of paper; neither did she come upon any broken bottles in the course of her wanderings. This lack seemed even more wonderful to her than the presence of innumerable foxgloves. She had spent an occasional afternoon in the woods at Aberdour, but always in a crowd. Here the spaciousness and peace attracted her, even as it filled her little soul with an awe that was a thing apart from fear. If in after years Maggie should read what Mr. Henry James has written of "a great, good Place," she will understand it better than most people.

For the first week she met with no adventures. Her aunt, a bustling, busy, thrifty Scotswoman, worked a great deal up at the big house; her uncle assisted in the manufacture of the "superfine broadcloth" for which the little village used to be famous, and Maggie was left to do much as she pleased. Her cough left her, and the color came into her pale cheeks, and the sun set his mark upon the bridge of her nose in the shape of a band of the dearest little brown freckles.

Hitherto she had not gone far into the woods, but with returning health came a spirit of adventure. One afternoon she wandered on and on, singing softly to herself a ditty relating that "Kitty Bairdie had a coo," going on to describe minutely, and at length, the various animals owned by this worthy lady, and concluding each verse with the cheerful injunction, "Dance, Kitty Bairdie!"

Everything seemed to want to sing that afternoon, and did sing, too, lustily and long. Unconsciously Maggie raised her voice till the final "Dance, Kitty Bairdie!" had quite a rollicking sound, and she found herself doing a sort of double shuffle among the ground ivy and foxgloves.

It is not easy to dance in and out of ground ivy and brambles, and Maggie paused for breath, only to catch it again in a perfect agony of fear, as, not five yards from her, she beheld a big white figure, apparently just risen out of the ground.

Paralyzed with terror, she stood staring at the vision. A tall man it was—she was sure it was a man, and no ghost—clad in curious flowing robes of soft whitey flannel, falling to his feet in innumerable folds, while in his hand he held what Maggie took to be some instrument of torture. It was a butterfly net; but Maggie did not know this, for people did not catch many butterflies in Commercial Street, Leith.

The whole dreadful truth flashed upon her. This was one of the monks! Had she not read in a guide to the neighborhood that "The Dominican Priory of the Annunciation is a large and handsome building; here candidates for the priesthood pursue a course of study in divinity and philosophy. It is under the government of a Prior." This, then, must be one of the priests, and having been very well brought up in the strictest sect of the Free Kirk, she was sure that if only he succeeded in "catching her," she would be put to unspeakable tortures, or forced to recant her faith.

Had she not with her own eyes seen her mother hastily slam the door of their flat in the face of a woman wearing a queer head-dress and long cloak, who had come to beg for money?

"I'll ha'e none o' they Papishes here!" her mother exclaimed angrily, and then—for it was just before Maggie came south—"and you, Maggie, if you see ony o' them when you're wi' your aunty, just turn and flee. I'm told there's a whole clamjamfray o' them there, an' ye can never tell what they Jesuits will be at."

So, having found her breath sufficiently to give a wild cry, Maggie turned and fled.

The queer white man, who, as she afterward remembered, looked astonished, called something after her. But Maggie's heart was thumping in her ears to the exclusion of every other sound, and she ran blindly on till one treacherous little foot, more used to pavements than rough forest ground, gave under her with a horrid wrench, and she fell forward in a terrified little heap just as she reached a footpath leading she knew not whither.

There she lay shivering with pain and fear, with her eyes shut, for she heard the soft swish of long garments through the undergrowth. Then a shadow fell upon her, and she was lifted up into a pair of strong arms, while a voice that even her excited imagination could not construe as unkindly exclaimed:

"I do believe I frightened you, and I'm awfully sorry. I don't suppose you ever saw such a funny frock before!"

There was something human and disarming about the "awfully" and "funny frock"; moreover, the owner of the voice did not hold her as though she were a captive. He sat down at the foot of the big tree whose gnarled roots had tripped Maggie up, and set her on his knee. Besides, the voluminous flannel garment had a most reassuring and workaday smell of soap. But she could not bring herself to open her eyes just yet. She screwed them and her courage up very tight, and whispered:

"I'll no recant! Ye may burn me, but I'll no recant!"

The big, queer man threw back his head and laughed, and his laugh was even more inspiring of confidence than his speaking voice. But he pulled himself up short in the very middle of his laugh to ask:

"I say, though, did you hurt yourself when you fell?"

Maggie opened her eyes the tiniest little bit, and for the first time saw this queer man's face. It was a kind face, a handsome face, with large merry brown eyes and an exceedingly straight nose. His mouth was well cut and firm, and when he smiled as he did then, he showed two rows of admirably white and even teeth. And the good smell of soap was in no way deceptive, for there was about this queer man's appearance a radiant cleanliness that was by no means merely physical. All this did Maggie gravely take in through half-shut eyes, and though the pain in her ankle was horrible, and her heart still danced a sort of breakdown against her ribs, she was no longer afraid—only very, very curious.

The queer tall man, looking down at the face resting against his arm, noticed that it was small and white, with long-lashed closed eyes set rather far apart, and that the little freckles looked pathetically prominent across the thin small nose; and even as Maggie was comforted by the good smell of clean flannel, so he recognized approvingly that he held in his arms a very clean little girl, even though her pinafore was patched and her shoes worn at the toes.

"Are you hurt, you poor mite?" he asked again.

For answer Maggie stuck out the painful foot, and behold! there was a big lump on the ankle, and it looked twice as big as the other one.

"Here's a pretty kettle of fish!" cried the queer man. "You've sprained your ankle."

As he spoke he set Maggie on the ground beside him very gently, and diving into the folds of his habit produced a large handkerchief, which he proceeded to tear into strips. Then, very gently and deftly, he bandaged up the poor swollen foot. By this time Maggie's blue eyes were wide open, and as he stooped over her foot she found time to wonder why he wore such "a wee, wee roond cappie" on the back of his head. The pain was bad, but she tried hard not to flinch, and when it was all done and the bandage fastened with a little pebble brooch that she had worn at her neck, he said gaily:

"And now to carry you home, for that foot must have hot fomentations as soon as possible."

Here, however, Maggie demurred. "I can walk fine," she announced with great dignity, and tried; but it was no use—she couldn't even stand, the pain was so bad.

So the "papist man" picked her up in his arms and set off toward the village.

Now, Maggie was just a little anxious at this, for she had wandered a good way into the park, and the path he took seemed quite unfamiliar.

With unprecedented courage she took hold of his chin with her hand and turned his face that she could see it.

"You're sure you're no takin' me to your convent?" she asked gravely, as one who begs to know the worst at once. She still had fleeting visions of a dungeon followed by stake and faggots if she proved leal to the faith of her fathers.

"My dear child, they wouldn't have you there. We don't allow any women to come in—not even little girls—where I live."

Maggie was silent for a minute; then, because every Scotsman, woman, or child loves an argument, and a theological argument best of all, she said slowly:

"But you worship a woman—images of a woman."

"Ah, that's rather different. I don't think we'll discuss that, because, you see, we look at everything from rather different points of view. How's that poor foot of yours? You're a regular Spartan to bear pain. Am I carrying you comfortably?"

Here was another facer for Maggie; he did not want "to discuss that."

"I thought," she said, "that you liked to burn everybody wha' didna 'gree wi' you—when ye got the chance," she added.

"Oh, we're not quite so black as we're painted, and the world is big enough for us all nowadays, even though there are so many more people in it. Isn't that a good thing?"

Maggie's honest little heart yearned over this mistaken man, who carried little girls so tenderly, who seemed so kind and gay.

"I wish that you were no a papish," she said softly, "for I'm sorely afraid that ye'll no win Heaven if you worship graven images."

The papist in question stopped short in the middle of the woodland path. The sunlight shining through the leaves painted fantastic patterns on his white draperies, and his eyes were very kind as he said gently:

"Don't you think there will be even more room in Heaven than there is here for all sorts of people, provided they are kind, and brave, and honest, and do their best?"

And Maggie agreed that it might be possible, and was something comforted. By and by he asked her what the nice song was that she had been singing when he first met her, and she sang it again for him all through, till he, too, learned the tune; then she taught him the words, and although his Scotch left much to be desired, they made a very considerable noise between them, and the woods resounded to the strains of "Dance, Kitty Bairdie."

"They monks seem different to the ordinary sort," said Maggie that night, when, after much fomentation of the injured ankle, her aunt tucked her into bed.

"They're just harmless haverals," said her aunt indulgently; but Maggie "added a wee thing" onto her prayers, and whispered under the bed-clothes:

"Please make room for yon clean man at—any—rate."

COMRADES

He was called Bunchy because, when a very little boy, his clothes *would* bunch; the tiny petticoats were short for their width, and everything stuck out all round him like a frill.

Now that he was five, and wore breeches with four little buttons at the knee, the name still stuck to him, though it was no longer appropriate.

Bunchy was lonely.

If Pussy had been there it would have been very different; but she had been sent for quite suddenly to go and nurse dad, who had incontinently fallen ill with influenza just three days after mother (Bunchy always called her Pussy), Nana, and he had settled down for a fortnight's holiday in a Cotteswold village.

It was a delightful village! It had a green with noisy geese upon it, a stream that gurgled and splashed and told fairy tales on sleepy September afternoons, and real woods surrounded it.

The cottage where Pussy had taken rooms was ever so pretty, and had a garden full of currant-bushes and celery.

For three days they had a lovely time. They sought giants in the woods, finding squirrels instead—which were prettier and only less exciting; they paddled their feet in the stream and caught minnows in a bottle; they pretended that the geese on the green were "Trolls," and routed them with great slaughter; and they had found mushrooms before breakfast in a neighboring field.

Then Pussy had to go away, and for Bunchy the face of Nature was changed and clouded. Only Nana was left, and, although very kind, she was not an exciting companion. She knew nothing of giants, and seemed to care very little about Trolls. Moreover, on this particular morning she sat indoors making a cotton dress, and told Bunchy to "run and play in the garden like a good little boy, and not worry." How can people, he thought, sit in a room and sew when all the beautiful out-of-doors seems clamoring for them to come and admire it?

However, he played in the garden for a while; but it was rather a small garden, and he grew tired of being a "third son" all by himself, with no one to admire him, so he came in again and climbed the steep little staircase. Finding the door of his mother's room open, he went in. The dressing-table faced the door, and the first thing he saw was a pair of Pussy's slippers standing in front of it. They had tall curly heels and buckles, such as she loved, and he remembered how, even with the tall heels, she did not reach to daddy's shoulder. Somehow the sight of those slippers made him want her so dreadfully that he couldn't stay in the room or in the garden. He went out into the road to walk and walk until he should come to Yorkshire, where daddy was laid up in the house of a bachelor friend with whom he had gone to shoot.

It was a very straight road, with a trim path by the side. By and by he came to some big gates. There was a little house inside them, all covered with purple clematis. The gate stood open, and as Bunchy was rather tired of the neat, straight road, he turned in, and went down a very broad gravel path. A little way inside the gate stood two little churches, one on each side of the path; beyond them, as far as Bunchy could see, it was all garden. There were flowering shrubs, and trees, and lots of grass, but it was unlike any garden he had ever seen before, for it was full of little mounds, and there were crosses, and slabs of stone, and marble angels dotted about among the mounds.

He turned down a side-path to investigate further in this strange garden. Nobody was in sight, and he wandered on by himself till, turning a corner suddenly, he came upon a man.

The man was dressed in black, and was sitting on a big stone slab—a very grew old slab; but close at his feet there was one of those curious mounds that puzzled Bunchy, and although this one had no grass upon it, you could hardly see the brown earth, for it was almost covered with scattered flowers—all of one kind.

Bunchy knew the flower by sight, for Pussy always wore a bit in her tam-o'-shanter when she came back from Scotland. The man did not move as Bunchy came up to him. The little boy regarded him with grave brown eyes, and something in his expression made Bunchy sure that the man was sorry.

Now, in Bunchy's house, when people are sorry, Pussy talks about something else, and she does it so beautifully that they straightway forget their sorrow in the interest of her remarks. Bunchy felt that he ought to talk about something else to this man who looked so sorry; but how can you change a subject when no subject has been broached?

So the child went up to the sorry man and lifted his tam-o'-shanter, saying politely:

"Can you, please, tell me whose garden this is?"

Now it is an easy thing to take off a tam-o'-shanter, but when you try to put it on again it has a shabby way of curling up and sitting on the top of your head so insecurely that it topples off again directly. Pussy generally put Bunchy's on again for him, and as she wasn't there he left the matter alone and held it in his hand. The man started a little as Bunchy spoke, then he said slowly:

"I think it is God's garden."

Bunchy was not surprised. He felt that he knew God very well indeed. When you say prayers morning and evening, and know that there is a benevolent Somebody somewhere, who gives you your home, and your parents, and your little white bed, who likes you to be truthful and courteous, and to have clean hands at meals, it is quite natural to hear that this benevolent Person has a garden. All nice people ought to have gardens, so Bunchy said:

"Why does God have so many little rockeries in His garden? Why are there all these stones, and figures, and little mounds?"

"When people die they are buried in this garden, and their friends put up the crosses and stones——"

"And angels?" interrupted Bunchy admiringly; and as he looked up in the man's face he noticed that his eyes were very kind, but that there were big black shadows round them, and their lids looked red and heavy.

"They put up the crosses, and stones, and angels to show where their friends are sleeping," continued the tall man.

"Then it's a funeral," said Bunchy solemnly, and there was silence.

The man looked sorrier than ever, and Bunchy felt that now was the time to talk of something else, so he said:

"Can you tell me the nearest way to Yorkshire?"

The man seemed to give himself a shake, as though he were trying to wake up. He held out his hand to Bunchy, who placed his own in it confidingly; then he drew the child toward him and set him on his knee, asking:

"Why do you want to go to Yorkshire, old chap?"

"Because Pussy is there and I am so lonely," Bunchy's voice broke. "I went into her room, and I saw her shoes—the ones with the curly heels—and they made me want her so bad. They're such tall heels."

"She had such little feet," murmured the man.

And Bunchy saw that he had gone to sleep again, so he sat very still for a minute or two, then he said mournfully:

"I'm so lonely!"

"So am I," said the man. "My Pussy has gone to sleep. She is not coming back any more. She is sleeping under the heather here."

Bunchy felt the man's shoulder heave as he leant against him, but he said nothing. He felt that this was not a time to talk of something else; this sorryness was something beyond him; so he stroked the man's face with a soft, sticky little hand, and the corners of his mouth drooped, but he did not feel quite so lonely.

The man seemed to like the feel of the little hand, for he bent his head, and, laying his cheek against Bunchy's, said in a queer broken voice:

"How is it that you understand, you quaint little boy?"

"Sorry people always understand, and I feel to love you! Will you come to Yorkshire too? We should be such nice company."

The man seemed to consider; then he said:

"It's a long way. I'm afraid we shouldn't get there by candle-light. You'd be very tired, and your shoes would be quite worn out."

"Couldn't you carry me a bit sometimes? Daddy does when I'm very tired."

"Well, I might do that; but even then we shouldn't get there to-day. How is it you are here all alone?"

The man seemed waking up, and waited quite anxiously for Bunchy's answer.

"Well, you see, Nana was busy sewing, and I was lonely wivout Pussy, so I thought I'd walk to Yorkshire just to see her."

"Suppose you come to lunch with me instead. It's not so far as Yorkshire; still, it's a good way, and we'll go and tell Nana you're coming, then she won't be anxious. I don't think Pussy would like you to walk all that way to-day. She'll come back as soon as she can, you may be quite sure. Will you come? We'd be nice company, as you say."

Bunchy looked up into the man's eyes; then he slid off his knee, saying:

"I'll come, thank you."

The man got up off the big flat stone and held out his hand to Bunchy; but the little boy had knelt down by the mound all covered with heather. He stooped his curly head and kissed the flowers, saying in his sweet child's voice:

"Good-bye, man's Pussy! I hope you are happy in God's garden."

Then he took the man's hand and they walked away together.

But the man had gone to sleep again, for he said:

"Nay! And though all men, seeing, had pity on me, she would not see."

LITTLE SHOES

The Vicarage stands at the bottom of the market place, inside high walls and entered by wooden gates which generally stand open. Thus the passer-by can, for a moment, feast his eyes upon the perfect garden within.

The Vicaress was dead-heading her roses. She does this carefully every summer afternoon just after lunch. She had reached the bush of cabbage roses close to the gate, and her long lath basket lay on the drive beside her.

The market place was empty and still; nobody was shopping, for all the world rested preparatory to attending the Earl's garden-party later on. Road and houses alike glared white in the hot June sunshine, while in contrast the Vicarage garden seemed doubly cool and shady. The yew hedge just inside the gates threw long green shadows on drive and lawn. Such a lawn it was! Plantains or dandelions were a thing unknown. Other lawns might get brown or worn in a drought, but the Vicarage lawn was watered every night by a specially constructed hose, that the beauty of its velvet turf might never vary. The Vicar was wont to excuse his exceeding pride in his lawn by quoting: "The green hath two pleasures: the one, because nothing is more pleasant to the eye than green grass finely shorn; the other, because it will give you a fair alley in the midst." It was a sunken lawn surrounded by smoothly shaven banks and reached by broad stone steps.

The Vicar and like-minded clerics occasionally played bowls upon it; but to think of lawn tennis or croquet in connection with such grass were little short of sacrilege.

Presently the Vicaress became aware that a woman stood in the doorway, a woman carrying a baby, while a little girl of some three years clung to her skirts.

They stood gazing wistfully into the garden. As both mother and child wore red kerchiefs instead of hats, the Vicaress looked for the inevitable organ, but could not see it.

As she strongly disapproved of indiscriminate charity she shook her head at them, saying: "We never give at the door!"

Wearily shifting the baby to her other arm, the woman answered, with a touch of gentle dignity: "I have not ask the senora for money, but if she permit that we rest on the seat in the shade; we do no harm."

Her voice was soft, and her English refined by its foreign accent. The Vicaress pointed to a rustic seat under the yews, saying: "You may certainly come in and rest." Then she continued to deadhead the cabbage rose—it was an untidy bush that cabbage rose.

As the child toddled past her to climb into the seat the Vicaress noticed that the little feet made red marks on the gravel. The woman pointed to them with an apologetic shrug: "The little Zita she wear out her shoes, her feet bleed. The senora has a pair of old shoes of her children? Yes?"

The Vicaress shook her head, and a spasm of pain crossed her face. There were no children at the Vicarage now. But shoes? Yes! there were shoes. She bent down to look at the ragged little feet, and very gently took off Zita's shoes. "Her feet must be washed," she announced. "Will she come with me?"

Zita shook her curls out of her eyes, but on further inspection of the senora declined to budge. "Then I must bring the water here," said the Vicaress, marching away to fetch it.

She was a tall, thin woman, with keen grey eyes and a lined, hard face, framed in hair that Nature had intended to break into fluffy rings of sunlight round her brow. But the Vicaress coerced her hair with some abomination that kept it flat and close to her head. It was only when a shaft of sunlight struck the tight braid at the back that one realized it was of the true Titian color. She went up the wide oak staircase into her cool, sweet-scented bedroom, where the *Gloire de Dijon* roses nodded into the windows. Stopping in front of a big Chippendale wardrobe, she pulled out one of the deep drawers.

"I can't bear to do it!" she murmured, "but I never give money, and her little feet were cut and bleeding."

In that drawer lay many pairs of half-worn little shoes—shoes that had pattered gaily down the Vicarage stairs and danced across the sacred lawn. Her eyes were very soft as she chose out a pair of little strap shoes and some woollen socks. Had the Murillo cherub, chattering in her sweet jargon of Pyrenean Spanish under the shade of the yew trees, seen the face of the Vicaress just then, she would not have refused to go with her. But the Vicaress kept what Mr. Barrie tenderly calls her "soft face" for solitary places. The best that people could say of her was, that if her manner was hard her deeds were often kindly. She filled a basin with warm water and went through the silent house into the garden again. Zita laughed and showed her white teeth as she dabbled her feet in the water, becoming quite friendly; then the Vicaress dried her brown legs and arrayed her in the new shoes and socks. On the party being regaled with Vicarage cake and milk, the mother informed her hostess that they purposed to go on to Gloucester that day—a fifteen-mile walk.

"Have you no money to go by train?" asked the Vicaress.

"Oh, no, senora! My 'usban' sell ze ice cream there, he cannot send me large money."

"But you can't get there to-night; where will you sleep?"

The woman shrugged her shoulders, turning her unoccupied hand outward with an expressive gesture. "In the hedge, senora, it is cool and dry."

"But the children?"

"Oh, zay sleep—and Zita, she walk well till her foots come to ze ground." Then turning to the child she said something rapidly in Spanish, adding: "She sing for you, senora, you so kind for her."

"*A la puerta del cielos, venden zapatos,*" crooned Zita in her funny little nasal chant, and sang the lullaby right through.

"What is it all about?" demanded her hostess with a queer little catch in her voice.

"Senora! it is that zay sell shoes at ze doorway of heaven, to ze ragged little angels who have none!"

The woman rose, and shouldering the brown baby, prepared to depart. But the baby, who approved of Vicarage cake, choked alarmingly, and delayed matters for a while.

The baby's equanimity restored, they bade their hostess farewell. They had not gone very far, however, when hearing hasty footsteps behind them, they turned. It was the Vicaress. She thrust something into little Zita's hand, exclaiming breathlessly: "I wish you to go by train; it is not safe for such babies to be out all night!" Then she turned and fairly ran home.

An hour later, as she stood in front of her looking-glass, smoothing her hair till it looked like a yellow skull-cap, she said to herself: "To pay for a person's railway journey is not indiscriminate charity!" and her eyes grew tender as she thought of the little shoes.

"PASSING THE LOVE OF WOMEN"

"You sent for me, mother?"

"Yes, child; I sent for you to say good-bye. I am going away for some time." The woman spoke deliberately in the monotonous voice of one giving a piece of information tedious to give.

Angus did not express any surprise, or regret. The nine years he had spent with his mother had not helped him to know her. Without in the least understanding wherein lay her strange aloofness, he was conscious that he was supremely uninteresting to her. He wondered why it should be so, and his honest boyish soul was sometimes troubled. But children submit readily to the inevitable, and Angus had his compensations.

Vera Warden looked at her son with more interest than was usual with her. He was certainly a handsome lad, tall and well built, with blue eyes that were both kind and honest. She had been long in making her decision. Now that it was made she did not regret: she only wondered if, somehow, she had missed something that more commonplace women find easily.

"Angus, dear, you must take care of father. You and your father are so much alike—understand each other so well—that it will be easy for you. You must be especially good to him, now."

There was a curious little catch in Vera's voice as she said the "now."

"Why are you going, mother?" questioned Angus, feeling that here was something even more puzzling than usual in his mother's manner. "When are you coming back? Father will miss you."

"Will he?" asked Vera wistfully. "And you, Angus, will you miss me at all?"

Angus was profoundly astonished. He would like to have kissed his mother just as he kissed dad, but he did not dare. He only grew red, and fidgeted awkwardly, as he answered: "Of course I shall miss you, mother—at meals."

It was not greed that prompted the child's definition, but the fact that he seldom saw his mother, except at breakfast and lunch.

Vera Warden did not care for children, and said so—frequently.

The carriage came to the door, good-bye being said without much emotion on either side. As she was driven out of the big stone gates, Vera gave herself a little shake, saying: "And now for life!"

An hour later Thomas Warden returned from a fishing expedition on the other side of the Dale. The oak trees in the avenue had burst into gold-green leaf. The big chestnut on the lawn—the only chestnut on the estate—was covered with cones of pinky blossom. The May sunset touched the grim grey house with rosy light, and Thomas Warden felt a welcome in it all.

Laying down his rods and fishing-baskets in the hall, he went straight to his study. There on his blotting-book lay the letter he had both dreaded and expected.

His sunburnt face looked grey as he took it up. He sat down heavily; then, with shaking hands, opened the letter and read:

"I have burnt my boats; there is no going back. I warned you that it would come to this: that I would bear the monotony no longer. I have given you ten years of my life—the ten best years. Now I owe it to myself to live—it may be ten years more—but anyway, to *live*. Marriage and maternity have, for me, proved uninteresting; but I have endured them for your sake, and for the sake of the boy—while he was quite young. Had he been in any way an unusual boy I might have found life more tolerable. To develop his mind would have been an interest for me; he might have shared, in some degree, my aspirations after a fuller intellectual life. But he is a healthy, handsome, quite commonplace boy, who will grow into what you would call 'an honest, God-fearing man' without my help. He has an excellent governess, and your good mother will doubtless come frequently to worship you both. I wish I could free you of me altogether, and that you could marry again and be happy. But you are not the sort of man to bear with equanimity any sort of scandal or publicity, and you have my promise that the life I lead shall be such as can give you no cause for offence other than the fact that I lead it away from you. For your never-failing courtesy and kindness I thank you. Believe me, I shall always have the sincerest affection and respect for you. The fact remains, however, that I cannot lead your life, and you can lead no other. Let us then separate, and go our different ways in peace.

"In every conventional and actual sense, I am and will be your faithful wife,

"VERA WARDEN."

There was nothing in the letter that she had not said to him, many times, during the last six months.

Now, she had actually carried out her so often announced intention, and was gone; and the realization stunned him. He felt cold and numbed. The roar of the beck, in which he had stood all morning, was in his ears, and he gazed out into the gathering twilight, seeing nothing—only conscious that it was dark and chill everywhere.

There was a knock at the door, and a servant came in, saying: "Please, sir, Master Angus is ready, and would like you to come to him, if you are not too tired."

Dragging himself out of his chair, he passed his hand across his dazed, strained eyes. Then he went out of the room and up the wide old staircase to his dressing-room, where Angus slept.

"I've got a new nightsuit, dad, just like yours. Look—pocket and trowsies, and all!" exclaimed the child, displaying the latter garments with great pride. "Miss Taylor had them made for me in York. Aren't they nice?"

"Yes, my boy, yes—very!" but the voice was absent, and Angus felt that there was a something lacking, something that he generally found there.

The child felt frightened. Was dad, too, going to hold himself "aloof"? Would he, too, take to looking over people's heads, and answering in a far-away voice? The thought was one full of omen.

Angus gazed into his father's face, as he sat wearily on the edge of the little bed. The child, if commonplace, was quick to understand those who loved him. In a moment he acquitted his father, and came and knelt beside him, rubbing his curly head against his knees. He said his prayer with devoutly folded hands, as Grannie had taught him. Then, climbing into Warden's arms, put his own round his neck.

"Shall I sing my psalm, dad? Or are you too tired?"

His father held him very close. "Sing it, laddie. Sing Grannie's psalm."

Grannie was Scotch. When she came she taught Angus the psalms in metre. She taught him other things that he learned more easily than the psalms; chief among them a great love and trust in her, and through her, for everything Scotch.

Shortbread was Scotch, and it was good. Scones were Scotch, and they were good, especially with currants. Edinburgh rock was excellent; therefore the psalms, too, were probably superior in the Scotch version. Angus learned all Grannie's favorites, the first of which was the twenty-third:

My table thou hast furnished,

In presence of my foes.

The child always pictured a long table, covered with a fair white cloth, and plentifully plenished with plates piled high with scones and shortbread. He wondered what "foes" were, for he hadn't any; he thought they must be the servants who handed round the plates.

"Goodness and mercy all my life shall surely follow me." The sad, patient tune Grannie had taught him sounded almost triumphant, as the child's strong treble voice rang out. When he had finished, his father leant his head against the little rounded shoulder, and there was silence save for the man's quick breathing.

"Good-night, dad!" said Angus at last, turning himself to see his father's face.

Thomas Warden rose hastily; he laid the boy in his little white bed, kissed him, and blessed him, and went down and sat in the study again. But a man cannot dine in his fishing boots; so he went upstairs, had a bath, and while he dressed, Angus discoursed cheerfully to him through the half-open door.

The silence was unbearable; it was so lonely. Thomas Warden could not sleep. He got up and walked about his room. Only one o'clock! The night had hardly begun.

The moon shone brilliantly, but the wind blew shrewdly through the open casement. May nights are cold in the North country.

He went into the dressing-room and looked at Angus. "If she had only loved the boy—if she had only loved the boy." He could have forgiven her all the rest. A just and tolerant man, he knew his own limitations. He granted to the full his wife's intellectual superiority; but she might have loved the boy.

"Goodness and mercy all my life shall surely follow me." Why did those lines ring in his head? and then, there always followed the sentence in his wife's letter: "I cannot live your life, and you can live no other."

It was true: *he* could live no other. But the boy—why did she not love the boy?

He drew up the blind, and the mellow moonlight fell on the sleeping child. Surely he was a goodly child, so comely, and kindly, and honest. As he looked at the boy his heart went out to him. He did not stoop and kiss him as a woman would have done; he reverenced too much this fair sleep which wrapped him round. He went back to his own room and got a pillow. Then, laying his long length on the floor beside the little bed, and with the child's psalm still sounding in his ears, he too slept.

The room was flooded with moonlight when Angus awoke. There was a sound of regular and heavy breathing. Angus felt puzzled; puzzled, but not in the least afraid. Such breathing must come from a man, or a dog; from men and dogs the child had experienced nothing but kindness.

He sat up, and listening, looked about to see where the sound came from. He shook his hair back from his forehead, and rubbed his eyes. Yes! he was not mistaken, it *was* his father who lay there on the floor beside his bed.

Angus rose softly, and touched his father's bare feet; they were very cold. "Poor dad," he said to himself—"and him so tired!"

Then suddenly he remembered his mother's words: "You must take care of father." It was bad to sleep without a covering, Grannie had told him that. He pulled his little quilt off his bed, and laid it lightly on his father. To his delight the sleeping figure never stirred, but the quilt was short, and Thomas Warden was long—by no amount of stretching would it cover both his shoulders and his feet—poor cold feet! Then Angus was seized by an inspiration, which even his mother could not have called quite commonplace. He lay down at his father's feet, and unbuttoning the jacket of the new sleeping suit, he cuddled up so that the cold feet rested on his own warm breast. Then he, too, fell asleep.

The kindly moon shone in upon them, and it was very still.

When Thomas Warden awoke the moonlight had changed to pearly dawn. He was no longer cold, and when he realized why, he was no longer lonely.

A THROW BACK

Nana had at last gone out and left the coast clear. Kit seized her little brother's hand, and they sped down the long passage to the red baize door which swung heavily but did not latch, shutting off the nursery quarters from the house.

Kit was a person of dramatic instincts, and as they ran down the passage she quoted in a deep and awful voice, "The tiger is a fearful beast, He comes when you expect him least." Addison gazed fearfully over his shoulder, and ran at the top of his speed.

At last by a mighty effort they pushed open the heavy red door, and the staircase and the house lay before them for exploration. It was a very wide staircase, black and shiny and slippery, and as they went down their little feet made a pattering noise which seemed to echo and multiply in the silent house. Kit turned and said, "Hush!" in a reproving voice to Addison, who was, like Agag, walking delicately, on the banister side. "I can't hush any more than I'm doing!" he replied in an injured tone. "I must put my feet down firm or I'd skate!"

"Come on!" said Kit. "Let's go and see if Jakes is in the dining-room, and he'll tell us what's for lunch."

They crossed the stone-flagged hall, and Kit opened the dining-room door and marched boldly in. There was no one there; the big room was wrapped in silence, and Addison felt very small and timid as he stood on the threshold. Not so Kit; she walked boldly up to the table, which was laid. There was a great deal of old silver on the table, and many flowers; but its appearance was evidently most displeasing to Kit, for she exclaimed angrily:

"Look here, Addison, just look here! Jakes has only laid lunch for *one!*"

Even the mild and gentle Addison was roused to something like indignation at this tremendous intelligence. To have breakfast and tea in the nursery is an understood thing; but lunch—whoever heard of a well-conducted child having lunch anywhere but in the dining-room, once he or she could hold a spoon and fork? It was abominable; it had to be seen into at once.

Kit gave an indignant sniff, saying: "I know it isn't Jakes; it's Nana. She'd go and say we could have lunch with her till Miss Mercer came; but I'll go and speak to grandpapa at once; it's a shame; I won't stand it. Come on!"

The obedient Addison trotted after Kit across the hall with some alacrity. He hadn't seen much of grandpapa; but what he had seen he liked. How still the old house was, no sound to be heard but the drip, drip of the rain on the ivy outside the windows and the sizzle and fiz of the big logs in the great stone fireplace.

The children looked upon "Nanas" and their like as necessary evils. They divided mankind into two classes, which they called respectively "the dears" and "the deafs." To the "dears" belonged father and mother, all father's friends and most of mother's; Gaffer and all Gaffer's servants; orderlies— particularly orderlies—and grooms. To the "deafs" belonged nurses, governesses, cross gardeners, and a great many young ladies who wore smart frocks and were affectionate in public. These latter were called "deafs" not because of any defect in their aural arrangements, but simply because the children considered them incapable of discussing anything interesting. "Stupid people!" Kit was wont to observe, "who ask you how old you are, and who fetch stale cake out of tin boxes, and one's got to eat it for politeness' sake. Oh, I hate deafs!"

When Kit reached the study door she knocked, but there was no answer. "Mother says he never hears if he's writing," she whispered. "Let's go in— come on!" So she turned the handle of the door and went in. Grandfather was writing. His great knee-hole table was piled with open books, and he had on his gold-rimmed spectacles. He never looked up as Kit shut the door softly behind her. For one thing, doors never creaked in grandfather's house.

The children stood inside the door and waited, but he never looked up. "Come on," said Kit, as, holding Addison by the hand, they walked leisurely across the room, till she stood close by their grandfather; then she said in a loud and cheerful voice:

"Good-morning, Gaffer; we've come to see you!"

"We've come to see you!" echoed the ever-obedient Addison. Grandfather was fond of old-fashioned things, and the name "Gaffer" was so delightfully inappropriate that he encouraged the children to use it when they spoke to him.

"Oh, you've come, have you?" he said, taking off his spectacles and turning himself in his heavy revolving chair toward the children. "And how are you, my dears? Did you sleep well after your long journey?"

It did not take long to install a child on each knee. Addison gazed at him in adoring silence, but Kit hastened to unbosom herself of her wrongs. "I've come to complain!" she began with dignity. "They've only laid lunch for you in the dining-room. Now I know you'd like our company. Mother said we were to keep you company—will you give orders about it?"

Gaffer seemed duly impressed, as he said: "I will give orders at once. Of course you are to have lunch with me while you are here. It's a pity it's so wet for your first day, but it's nice to think that those dear people are going further and further away from the fogs and damp. It will do mother so much good to be in a warm climate, and you must try not to feel dull without them."

"I wish they'd taken me!" said Kit. "I love hotels!" Gaffer looked at her and laughed: "What a traveled little person you are! I never slept in a hotel till I was seventeen."

"Ah, but that's long ago. People go about more now, and, you see, we have to go with the regiment."

"To go with the regiment," echoed Addison.

Kit conversed affably with her grandfather for some time; she told him who were her favorite officers, and which her favorite puddings. She carefully explained that, as she was four years older than Addison, she went to bed an hour later, and that she intended to spend that hour in her grandfather's society. She expressed her approval of the study as a room, but thought it was a pity that, owing to the large number of books, there was no space for any pictures on the walls. Addison stared about him in solemn silence, till at last Gaffer suggested that, as he had got to write to mother, they had better go back to the nursery till lunchtime. Then they trotted across the room together, but when they reached the door and Kit had gone out, Addison raced back and stood by his grandfather's chair, whispering breathlessly: "Will you let me see some of the books some day—wivout Kit?" There was a passionate eagerness in the question which startled Gaffer. He looked down at the imploring, upturned face.

And then "a strange thing happened." It was no longer Addison, his namesake, that he saw; it was himself. Himself of sixty years ago. There he stood, the quaint, serious-eyed boy, whose portrait hung in his dead wife's dressing-room. The boy who longed for books, and who had asked the same question of a scholar in an Oxford library, on a long-forgotten morning all those years ago. With a sudden rush of gratitude he remembered how the question had been answered, and though his smile was very pleasant, his voice was a trifle husky as he said:

"Assuredly!"

"Wivout Kit?" persistently questioned the little boy.

"Without Kit, I promise," repeated Gaffer. Then he and Addison shook hands, and Addison followed Kit.

She was waiting in the hall. "What did you say to Gaffer?" she asked inquisitively, but Addison shook his head. He could keep his own counsel even when coerced by pinches.

At lunch Gaffer inquired: "Addison, can you read?"

"Not well!" answered Kit. "He can't read well; he's only doing 'sequel,' and he's six. He's very backward!"

"I asked Addison, my dear," said Gaffer, in gently reproving tones.

Addison blushed and held down his head; then he said: "I don't like what I read; it's so uninteresting. They ask such silly questions, over and over again."

"He knows heaps of poetry!" said Kit magnanimously. "He can learn anything when he's heard it once, and he knows pages of verses, and psalms, and that, but he's no good on horseback. He's got no nerve. Dad says he'll never be any good across country! And he's afraid of the dark!"

"Are you not nervous?" asked Gaffer.

"Me nervous!" said Kit with great scorn. "I can ride dad's chargers!"

"Ah, you're like your mother," said Gaffer, smiling at her. "Now I, I was never any good across country; but yet I haven't found that it has alienated my friends, or done me any great damage in life. Has Addison begun Latin?"

"Oh, no; Miss Mercer doesn't teach Latin, and he's far too backward in other things to begin."

"I began Greek when I was his age," said Gaffer dreamily; "but there's no reason why Addison should not begin Latin. He shall begin it with me."

Addison flushed up to the roots of his hair; then he scrambled off his seat— a most unheard-of proceeding in the middle of lunch—and ran round to his grandfather. He threw himself upon him, exclaiming: "I love you; oh, how I love you!"

Kit regarded him with astonished eyes. That Addison, who never kissed anybody but mother, who was so undemonstrative, so slow to show feeling, should behave in this extraordinary manner, because he was told he might have Latin lessons, was to her incomprehensible; and Gaffer seemed to approve, for he lifted Addison on to his knee, and said in such a queer voice: "I think we're rather of a kidney, you and I; we're going to understand each other uncommonly well," and Addison sat enthroned on Gaffer's knee all the rest of lunch, and shared his cheese. Kit felt injured.

When Gaffer went back to his study he sat down before the fire, and he pondered for a long time over his queer little grandson. Then he gave his shoulders a shake and sighed: "I was a disappointment to my father, and he'll be a disappointment—he is a disappointment—poor little chap, to his. He is unaccountably like me."

A lonely child was Addison. The fact that he was always called Addison from the time he ceased to be baby was proof enough. A child who is understood gets a nickname. Kit had fifty. Addison was always called by his baptismal name. It was Gaffer's name, and Gaffer's grandfather had been called after a gentleman who wrote poetry and things. Little Addison knew that much, and he wondered if the writings of that far-away Mr. Addison were more interesting than "Step by Step." Addison was called an "old-fashioned child"; he was not very sure precisely what that was, but that it was something a child ought not to be, he was convinced. Kit was pretty, very pretty; so the officers said, not infrequently to Kit herself. Kit was never afraid of anything by day or by night. Kit always spoke the truth; Addison had been known to prevaricate when he was frightened, and he was often frightened—at nothing at all, Kit said.

But the worst and most unforgivable thing about Addison was this: he had no wish to be a soldier—and said so. The sound of a pop-gun caused his heart to thump against his breast in an unpleasantly violent manner, and a review was to him a prolonged agony that made him ill for days.

His mother—whom he worshipped—and who loved him tenderly, was quite unconscious of his many sufferings. She was absolutely devoid of nerves herself, and thought that Addison would grow out of his "delicacy," as she called it. She was proud of his remarkable resemblance to her father, whom she admired above all mortal men—but she was disappointed; and poor Addison, with the quick intuition of childhood, was perfectly aware of it— at his being what her husband called "such a Molly."

So it came about that Kit was always brought forward, and Addison kept in the background—to his own satisfaction certainly, but very much to the detriment of Kit.

Edinburgh, where the regiment was stationed, was too cold for mother, and dad obtained leave to take her to the Riviera for the worst months; so Kit and Addison were sent to Gaffer, and for Addison it was the turning-point of his life.

To most people, their initiation into the accidence of the Latin language is not a very happy recollection. To Addison it is a recollection little short of rapturous.

To him the first pages of a Latin grammar call up the picture of a large, old-fashioned room, flooded with a mellow light like that of the sun through a veil of yellowing beeches. There is a goodly smell in the room, the smell of dressed and well-kept leather. The walls are lined with books, books bound in calf and russet-colored Russia, and in the middle of the room stands a knee-hole table both deep and wide. It, too, is covered with books; but here they lie open, one upon the other, a crowd of witnesses to the tastes of the owner of the room. That gracious owner! Addison's eyes grow dim as he thinks of the spare upright figure seated in the revolving chair; the keen scholarly face and noble white head. He hears again the kind, cultivated voice ever ready to answer questions, to answer them so fully and so beautifully, with such a tender sympathy for the eager childish questioner. And then Addison goes down on his mental knees and thanks his God that as yet he had brought no look of sorrow into those kind eyes, but many a look of pride and joy.

Is there not one shelf in that library devoted to Addison's prizes? And the row is lengthening by leaps and bounds. Yet they wonder at Winchester why he should be so fond of classics.

THE INTERVENTION OF THE DUKE

I
ENTER WIGGINS

The Reverend Andrew Methven stood at his study window gazing out to sea. The sea was very blue, the sands yellow and smooth, but it was not the sea that the Reverend Andrew saw.

Elgo, on the Fife coast, is growing fashionable. In summer every house is let, and there are sometimes as many as fifty bathers at once in the bay. At Elgo the bathers usually wear blue serge, adorned it may be by red or white braid. Pale blue silk with white facings and short sleeves is not the usual uniform. It impressed the Reverend Andrew, and consequently he stood and stared. Moreover, the wearer of this wonderful creation—he felt it was a "creation," though he had never heard the word so used—came out of the house next door to the Manse, the house being that of his most worthy parishioner, Mrs. Urquhart, Baker and Confectioner, who let her rooms during the summer months.

Elgo streets are somewhat one-sided, the town being built upon the cliff with a railing near the outer edge for the protection of the unwary.

The vision in pale blue silk tripped down the steep steps cut in the rocks, and ran across the sands. She was followed by a small thin boy, whose freckled face was broad and good-natured. On the sands they took hands and danced into the water together.

The vision was tall and slim, with wonderful arms that flashed white in the June sunshine, and the minister remarked that she could swim magnificently. The little naked boy splashed after her, looking like a terrier as he shook the water from his crop of curly hair.

The minister's window was open, and across the sunlit sands came the sound of a woman's voice, crying: "Come on, Wiggins, get on my back, and I'll swim with you to the Cock's-tail Rocks!"

The Reverend Andrew swung his telescope into position; he had the grace to blush as he did so, but none the less did he eagerly follow that swimmer by its aid. She did it, there and back; then she and the small boy ran dripping over the sands and vanished through Mrs. Urquhart's side door.

An hour later the minister (he was the Free Kirk minister really; there is an Established Church in Elgo, but as its pews are empty and its incumbent of small account, he was "the minister" to Elgo) strolled into Mrs. Urquhart's shop to buy cookies. Mrs. Urquhart herself bustled forward to serve him.

"You've let your rooms, I see, Mrs. Urquhart! And early in the season, too!"

"Yes, sir! I've let my rooms, and to my own young lady that I was nurse to; you'll mind my telling you of Sir John Penberthy and his bonny family. Well, Mrs. Burton is just my Miss Mary, married and widowed too, poor lamb, and she and Master Wiggins have come all the way from London to be with me, and it's proud I am to have them!" Mrs. Urquhart paused breathless.

The minister murmured something sympathetic, and taking up his bag of cookies strode back to the Manse. "Mary, mother of names," he thought, as he turned over the information he had received. "Widowed! She doesn't wear much mourning anyway!" as he thought of the blue silk bathing-dress. Then he said with a sigh, "She is very beautiful!" and sat him down to write his Sunday sermon.

In the afternoon he met Wiggins on the beach: that gentleman was digging while a French *bonne* kept guard in the rear.

"Do you like Elgo?" asked the minister. He had a kindly way with children; he was rather childlike himself, and they knew it.

"Awfully," answered Wiggins, patting his castle walls, and barely looking up.

"Have you ever been to the sea before?"

"Oh, dear, yes; haven't you?"

"I live here," said the minister, rather discomposed by this exceedingly cool child.

"I wish I did!" sighed Wiggins. "I hate Kensington."

"Ah, that's London! I've never been there," said the minister simply. "I wish I had."

"It's not a very nice place. There's gardens and busses, and sometimes we ride in a hansom, and you always have to wear your shoes and generally gloves, it's beastly." Wiggins spoke bitterly, as one who had tasted the hollow shams of Kensington.

The minister sat down on the sand.

"Isn't there a museum there, and an Art Gallery?" he asked.

"Oh, yes, but you mayn't touch anything, and you have to wear your hat!"

"You seem to object to clothing," remarked the minister.

"Don't you?" responded this discomposing child.

"Well, no, I can't say I do. It's warm, and——"

"Oh, it's warm enough in Kensington, if that's what you want!" and Wiggins turned to dig a fresh channel from his castle to the sea.

"M'sieu Wiggins, il faut aller à la maison pour le thé. Faites vos adieux à M'sieu le Curé!" and Madeleine, the pretty French *bonne*, folded up her crochet, and rose.

But Wiggins was smitten with deafness, and waded deeper into the water, with a seraphically unconscious look.

Madeleine went down to the water's edge, where she discoursed volubly for about five minutes. The minister sat watching; he wondered why French people speak so fast, and whether Wiggins understood. He evidently did, for he answered derisively, and sat down suddenly in the water. Then he came out, and grinning at the minister, remarked gleefully as he took his dripping way homeward:

"That's the third pair to-day, soon shan't have any left to wear. What a rux!"

"So that's a London child!" mused the minister. "He's a fine frank lad; I must call upon his mother."

II
A NEW ATMOSPHERE

But the days went on, and the minister did not call. He was a sociable fellow, much beloved by his fisher folk, and by such summer visitors as knew him. Elgo was his first "charge." Had he been small, instead of six-foot-three, he would doubtless long ago have been dubbed "The Little Minister," after Mr. Barrie's immortal hero, for he was young as a minister can be.

He did not call on Mrs. Burton because he had conceived for her an extravagant admiration, or rather adoration. He met her constantly on the beach and in the village street, and on these occasions gravely lifted his hat. Had he followed his impulse, he would have gone down on his knees and begged leave to kiss her feet. We do not follow our impulses in these matters nowadays, and Mary Burton never wondered why he did not call, for she thought about him not at all.

She did not go to church that first Sunday, but played with Wiggins on the beach all the morning. Mrs. Urquhart was scandalized and suggested the Episcopalian church at Pittenweem; but Mary only put her arms round her old nurse and laughingly promised to come and sit in her pew next Sunday.

The minister progressed in his friendship with Wiggins; while Mary was scouring the country on her bicycle, Wiggins and his new friend played on the beach or fished for poddlies from the rocks.

Madeleine with the inevitable crochet sat on the beach and beamed at them.

"You're a Presbyterian, aren't you?" asked Wiggins abruptly of the minister one afternoon.

"Yes, I'm a member of the Free Kirk."

"Oh, you're Free Kirk, and Madeleine's a Roman Catholic, and mother and me is Pagans!"

"Pagans?" echoed the minister in astonished tones.

"Well, mother says so. It means that you love the sun, and the sea, and bare feet and meringues and music-halls and things!"

"Pagans, music-halls!" The minister gazed in horror at the unconscious but breathless Wiggins. "Do you mean to say," he asked solemnly, "that you do not know anything about our Saviour who died for us?"

Wiggins turned and looked at him with something of reproachful scorn on his broad freckled face; then he said slowly: "Of course, I know, but we never talk about *that* to strangers, mother and me. It is bad form, like the people who give you tracts in busses."

"I beg your pardon, I misunderstood," said the minister.

They were silent for a few minutes, during which the minister digested this, to him, new view of confessing your faith before men.

Although he himself never gave tracts either in busses or anywhere else, he had certainly in a sort of hazy fashion considered that to do so was praiseworthy, if mistaken.

"There's mother!" announced Wiggins suddenly. "Let's come and talk to her."

The minister scrambled to his feet, and in another moment he had shaken hands with Mrs. Burton, and they all sat down on the beach together.

Wiggins did most of the talking, and then it began to rain.

"Will you come in and have a cup of tea with Wiggins and me?" asked Mrs. Burton.

The minister felt that no words at all expressed the rapture with which this proposal filled him.

Mrs. Urquhart's parlor looked so different that afternoon. Many photographs stood on the mantelpiece, books other than albums or Family Bibles were scattered on the table, papers and magazines strewed the horsehair sofa, while on the mantelpiece among the photographs and the little vases full of roses were the ends of many half-smoked cigarettes. Another shock was in store for the minister.

They had tea; he drank three cups and ate endless scones in order to prolong the meal. To sit opposite to Mary and watch her white, heavily ringed hands flit in and out among the cups as she made tea was a wonderful thing. To listen to her as she praised Elgo, and Scotland generally, in her soft Southern voice was wonderful; but most wonderful of all was to gaze at her unrebuked, to drink in the beauty of her face, to note the gracious line of cheek and chin as she turned her head, and lose himself in the depths of her eyes, brown as the trout stream beyond Glen Dynoch. When at last some small consciousness of material things awoke in him and he rose to go, Mary reached to the chimneypiece for a slim tin box.

"Will you have a cigarette?" she asked. "Dear Mrs. Urquhart forgives my evil habits, and pretends she thinks that I smoke for asthma. I don't look asthmatical, do I?"

"Thank you," faltered the minister. "I do not smoke now—I gave it up after my student days, just as I gave up drinking anything, for the sake of my people. I daresay it was useless, but I thought it was right—then."

He spoke diffidently, humbly, half expecting a flash of amused scorn in her, such as he not infrequently encountered in Wiggins. But Mary held out her hand, saying softly:

"I am sure it was right then, and is now; but don't judge me hardly, for I have no flock to influence. My boys will smoke, anyhow, when they are big."

"It is kind of you not to laugh at me," he said, and with that took his leave.

Mary lit her cigarette and smoked thoughtfully for some time. Wiggins was once more searching for treasure on his beloved beach. She sat at the open window and watched the boats come in. Presently she rang the bell for Mrs. Urquhart. When that good lady appeared, breathless from her ascent of the steep little stairs, Mary pushed her into an armchair and sat down at her feet, with her head against the old woman's knees.

"Amuse me, nursey; tell me about your minister. Where does he come from? How is it that, without having been anywhere or seen anything, he is such a perfect gentleman, and why—oh, why is he a Free Church minister?"

"And what for no, my dearie? He's an excellent, well-doing young man. You should hear him preach; it's just wonderfu'. His father's a doctor near Aberdeen; bein' douce people they are—a large young family, and all doing well. He was at the college in Edinburgh, and passed very high. But it's no his learning that we care about, it's his kind, friendly ways. He'd take his turn nursing a body that's sick just like one of the family; and he's just a wonderful way with young men. To be sure, he's young himself—only just twenty-six— but he's not a bit bumptious or puffed up, like many young men. He's greatly set up with Master Wiggins; they're grand friends."

"He has been very kind to Wiggins. I'll ask him to dinner. Will you cook me a very nice dinner, nursey dear, on Thursday evening?"

"He'll no come then, my dearie, for it's prayer-meeting night. I just wish you'd go yourself."

"I've never been to a prayer-meeting. What's it like? What happens?"

"It's just beautiful, my dearie; and the gentry go too. Mrs. Braid, of Elgo House, she always goes."

Mary made a little face. "She called upon me yesterday. I didn't find her very exciting. I've got to dine there to-night, so I suppose I must dress. You might send Madeleine to do my hair. Dear nursey, I'd far rather stay with you than go to Elgo House."

III
"ALL SECRET SHADOWS AND MYSTIC SIGHTS"

Dinner parties at Elgo House were not, as a rule, exciting. The conversation generally vibrated between the harvest prospects and the game prospects, with somewhat numerous flashes of silence, during which each guest madly racked his brain for a fresh topic of conversation, only to fall back finally upon the weather.

Andrew Methven did not expect to enjoy himself much on that particular evening. His presence at Elgo House was something of an anomaly, for the family were "established" by conviction, yet Mrs. Braid attended the Free Kirk because she liked Andrew's sermons.

He felt rather as though he were poaching on his neighbor's preserves when he went there. He liked his brother cleric (as he liked most people), who, if old and somewhat dull, was kindly and human. So long as his evening pipe and toddy were forthcoming with regularity the "established" minister recked little if he preached to empty benches. Andrew Methven felt the blood rush to his face as on entering the Braids' drawing-room he heard that voice which had been ringing in his ears ever since his parting with Mary that afternoon.

Daylight lasts long in the North Country, and there were no candles needed at Elgo House for dinner. Mary sat opposite the minister, and had he been given to cursing he would have cursed the tall epergne of fruit that hid her from his sight, especially as the majority of her remarks were addressed to him.

The only other guests were an elderly colonel and his wife, who were staying at the hotel. The colonel, whenever he looked at or spoke to Mary, seemed by his very atmosphere to ejaculate "Monstrous fine woman," and Andrew felt an insane desire to choke him there and then in his own high white collar.

Dinner over, they all strolled into the garden, and then that happened which made an epoch in Andrew Methven's life.

When they had all duly admired the roses and the goodly promise of peaches on the south wall, someone brought a guitar out of the house and Mary sat down to sing.

Her dress, some soft transparent blackness over white, faded into the shadows among which she sat. Somehow it reminded Andrew of the silver birch trees in the copse beyond. She bent her head as she tuned the guitar, and the throb of the strings seemed an appropriate background to the sweetness of her profile. Vision and sound became indissolubly mixed. Andrew could never afterward separate Mary's face from her voice, and both were irresistibly a part of the beech copse seen dimly in the evening light. The whole making a picture, subtle, detached, vivid; an experience in which all the senses bore an equal part and were indistinguishable.

Mary's voice was a big, soft contralto, as unlike the usual "drawing-room voice" as it is possible to be, and she sang seriously. She gave her message to the four winds to be carried where they listed. She sang to the scented night, to the distant sea, to the flowers and the moonlight: not to the little handful of human beings, whose chairs creaked as they sat, and who, saving one, only realized that she was a beautiful woman who had a fine voice.

They thanked her when she had finished, all but Andrew, who, white-faced and dumb, gazed into the deepening shadows as he stood by Mary's chair.

"It's really most extraordinary to be able to sit out at night in June in Scotland, is it not?" said the colonel's wife in his ear. He started, looking at her stupidly. "A very absent young man!" she said to herself.

Truly he was absent, for he had been in heaven.

Mary, too, was silent, softly beating out a faint melody on her guitar as it lay across her knees.

Suddenly she looked up at Andrew, saying under her breath: "The rest may reason and welcome, 'tis we musicians know!"

"The rest" did not hear, or hearing did not understand; but Andrew said: "Thank God!"

The colonel's voice was heard declaring that it was "deucedly chilly," and everybody made a move to go indoors, except Andrew, who, pleading work, fled down the drive, only to walk for miles aimlessly in a direction leading further and further from the Manse.

Had he but known it, that walk was symbolical of the rest of his life. When he did get home his rather ancient "evening shoes" were quit worn out.

IV
THE EDUCATION OF THE MINISTER

"The Duke is coming at the end of the month," announced Wiggins to the minister, as they anchored and fished for poddlies in the bay.

"What Duke?"

"My brother; he's at school at Leamington; he's going to Eton in three years. He's ten, four years older nor me." Wiggins was a model of conciseness in the way he imparted information.

"Why do you call him the Duke?" asked the minister in rather an abstracted voice; he was watching a tall lady on the distant links.

"'Cause he is one; his name's Marmaduke, and he is a tremenjous Duke; they all say so."

"Who are *they*?"

"Oh, mother, and uncles, and boys, and people."

"Is he like you?"

"Not a bit; he's handsome; he's exactly like mother."

The minister smiled. Was Mary handsome? he wondered. For many days now he had forgotten to take her beauty into account. He never compared her with other women. She was not to him more beautiful, not more clever, not more kind than other women; she was simply what that Frenchman said of his lady—she was *mieux femme*. There was no one else.

"Are you very fond of your brother?" asked the minister, forcing himself to attend to Wiggins.

"I'm glad he goes to school," replied that gentleman guardedly. "He rather bangs me about."

"Is Wiggins a family name?" abruptly demanded the minister.

"You *are* a jokey man," said Wiggins admiringly. "Why, it's because of my hair they call me that; my name's Tregenna—'Tre, Pol, and Pen,' you know. Mother's Cornish."

At this moment Wiggins had a bite, therefore excitement reigned for the next five minutes, and even the advent of the Duke was forgotten.

Did Mary Burton know what she was doing when she admitted this obscure Free Kirk minister to friendship and intimacy? Did she realize how contact with her kindness, her simplicity, her gentlehood, was making him every day more hopelessly her slave? In after years, when he walked in darkness, with a hunger that nothing appeased, Andrew would ask himself this question, and whichever way he answered it he blessed her. He no more thought of blaming her than the sailor thinks of tracing the storm to the evening star.

"She shall have worship of me," he said in those early days of wonder and happiness. "She still has worship of me," he said after years of unsatisfied longing and ceaseless pain.

There was a song that Mary used to sing, a song he loved, written by a man for whom and for whose writings in those youthful opinionated days Andrew felt a hatred that was almost fear. Yet the song dominated him, and in after years he would repeat it to himself with a curious fierce sense of possession.

O brother, the Gods were good to you.

Sleep, and be glad while the world endures.

Be well content as the years wear through;

Give thanks for life, and the loves and lures;

Give thanks for life, O brother, and death,

For the sweet last sound of her feet, her breath,

For gifts she gave you, gracious and few,

Tears and kisses, that lady of yours.

Again across the silence he would hear Mary's voice; again would he see against the evening sky her delicate pale profile and the little head weighted with its coils of shadowy hair; accompanying it all, the soft plash of the waves as they rolled over the sands beneath her window and the sharp salt wind which sighed foreboding things.

"No! I won't sing any more to-night; let us talk," said Mary.

The weather had turned unkindly, a bright fire flickered on the hearth, while the rain outside drove and pattered against the rattling windows. The minister had come in "for some music" as had become his habit during the last weeks, but, Mary was in no mood to sing, so she laid the guitar aside.

"You told me that you intended to criticize my sermon of yesterday," said Andrew deferentially. "I gather that you altogether disagree with me."

Mary lit a cigarette and smiled at him, her own indulgent smile, which always softened the severity of her remarks. "Yes, I think your view is narrow, and in some respects unjust. Of course, I know it is the kind of sermon that is popular; and it is certainly kind to the novelists to abuse them from the pulpit—it increases the sale of their books so enormously. But that was hardly your object, was it?"

"I do not know what was my object, unless it were to deliver a message that I felt had been entrusted to me. I do feel strongly on this question. It seems to me so pitiful that people should waste their time in reading injurious trash, when all the time there waits in silent patience the great company of the Immortals."

"I like Schumann's view best. He says, 'Reverence what is old, but have a warm heart also for what is new.' Much that is new is true, and beautiful, and helpful."

Mary leant forward, looking eagerly through a little cloud of smoke at the minister.

He shook his head. "A great deal is hopelessly false, and ugly and lowering."

"I think you overrate the influence of bad books," said Mary. "It is only the great books that live; a meretricious book may have a few months' popularity, and then no one reads it any more, it is forgotten as absolutely as we forget the smell of decaying cabbage when we have passed the rubbish heaps."

"But surely you will allow that there is a great badness as well as a great goodness. Look at those Frenchmen; you cannot say their work is good, but it certainly will live, because it is great."

The minister spoke earnestly. He hated that she should think him narrow; but he had the courage of his opinions.

Mary was silent for a minute, then she looked at him and smiled, saying frankly:

"That is true; but I believe that in all genius there must be something of goodness. We are all going to heaven, and De Maupassant is going too."

"I would like to think they are all going, but it seems to me some of them have much to answer for. Influence is an awful responsibility. I believe it is the one thing for which we shall have to give the strictest account."

Mary looked grave. "Do you think that people always realize when they have influence?"

"No, not always; they do not certainly realize the extent of their influence. You, for instance, were you less noble-minded, might do incalculable harm, for you never think about the effect you produce at all."

"Oh, please don't be so seriously complimentary," she exclaimed. "To pose as 'a good influence' would be too dreadful! I should feel like seven curates rolled into one. Confess now, though, that you always thought a liking for cigarettes was the sign in a woman of moral obliquity, now, didn't you?"

Andrew blushed. "I have seen very little, and known few interesting people," he said modestly; "none from your world."

"How far we are getting from your sermon on modern literature; that is what we were going to talk about."

"I spoke as I felt; I daresay I am wrong, but I can't feel wrong yet. It may be that I overestimate the influence of books; but you see, in my case, books have been the only great influences I have known—until lately," he added softly.

Mary looked into the fire in silence for a few minutes, then she said: "Never judge a man by one book any more than you would judge him by one single act, but be grateful when you come across any piece of work that you like. It always seems to me that we render so little gratitude to the people who give us so much pleasure, and it must be sad for them."

She threw the end of her cigarette into the fire, and stood up, holding out her hand.

"I must send you away, for it's half-past ten, and we are early folk here."

Andrew bowed over the fair kind hand, and went back to his study at the Manse. Here there was no fire, no genial smell of smoke, everything was orderly, cold, and dull. Andrew sat down by his writing-table, and laid his head down on his arms. Truly the thoughts of youth are long, long thoughts.

A sleepless night is interminable at six-and-twenty. At forty, one takes it as something that has to be got through, probably with the aid of chloral.

V
MARY

There are people who can stir up the worst that is in us; that strange, inherent moral obliquity, which few are so happy as to be without, but which most of us bury under our strivings after things lovely and of good report. When success crowns the efforts of these moral dredgers, and they are generally as successful as they are persevering, they stand aside, apparently aghast, and proceed to cry "shame" noisily upon our depravity. These are they who "compound for sins they are inclined to" by damning, not "those they have no mind to," but such sins as at the time they happen to be tired of.

There are others, thank God for it, with whom intercourse is a sort of festival, not merely because their own outlook is so generous and kindly, but because they rouse what is best in one's self. One leaves such friends—they are friends if you have met them once—strong and gay and full of belief in the infinite possibilities of life.

Mary Burton was of this latter class. She made no great sacrifices, she enjoyed her life thoroughly, taking eagerly all pleasure that came in her way; but her temper was generous, her mind broad, and because she herself could not understand meanness, she never suspected others. She was seldom disappointed. It is the narrow little soul who so constantly encounters other narrow souls. The simple, kindly people meet with simplicity and kindness.

Perhaps the fact that their outlook was so similar proved the great bond between Mary and the minister of Elgo. Their upbringing and environment were so absolutely dissimilar, their views of life so unlike, yet beyond it all and through it all sounded the same note, dominating the discords and making harmony.

"He's such a lovable good fellow," Mary would say to herself. "One forgives him for always using shall and will in the wrong places, and for denying himself everything that some people think makes life endurable."

"She is so kind and gracious, so dignified without being haughty, so absolute an aristocrat in all her beautiful ways; she is a princess. What does it matter if she does smoke and read French novels? If she does it, it must be right for her." So argued the minister, though he kept his own sturdy Scottish opinion with regard to the unwholesomeness for ordinary digestions of some of the literature which Mary affected.

So the days went on and these two lovable good people saw more and more of one another, worshipper and worshipped, and although the parties mainly concerned preserved the ostrich-like blindness of people in their condition, the "summer visitors" of Elgo and the parish itself took a lively interest in their doings and waited with a somewhat impatient expectation of the climax.

One thing struck Andrew Methven as curious: in all their many conversations Mary had never mentioned her husband. She talked frankly of her father and her brothers, of the people she had met in India, and of those she was in the habit of meeting in London, but of her husband, never. Andrew found himself wondering what manner of man Captain Burton had been; but it never occurred to him to try to find out anything about Mary or her surroundings. He never spoke of her to anyone, and winced if anyone spoke of her to him. About his own family and his own "past," if so uneventful life can be said to have a past, he was most frank.

"My people are what you would call 'nice middle-class' people, perhaps a little fonder of books than their sort are in England, but you have never met anybody of that kind except me, and you would not find them congenial."

Mary made a little face. "I'm sure I never spoke of anybody as a 'nice middle-class person,' I shouldn't be such a snob, and I have met all sorts of people—people you would think Bohemian and terrible!"

"I should like to meet literary people," said Andrew wistfully, "but I suppose I never shall."

"Oh, yes, you will, and you won't find them any more interesting than your Fifeshire fisher folk. Epigrams pall upon you when they form the staple commodity of conversation. The somewhat dingy journalist, who has a trick of smart talking and who poses to himself as everything he is not, is just as great a bore as the respectable city clerk who lives at Hornsey and expatiates upon its advantages. You must not mistake cleverness for genius. The one is often merely the result of environment and atmosphere. The other nearly always appears in unlikely and seemingly impossible places. You know what Swinburne says: 'There is only one thing we may reverence, and that is genius. There is only one thing we may worship, and that is goodness.'"

"It seems to me," said Andrew thoughtfully, "that you reverse it. You reverence goodness and worship genius!"

"Perhaps I do, certainly and perhaps fortunately, the one is much rarer than the other. The best things in life are the commonest. There are flowers, and children, and love, and friendship for everybody, if they will have them."

"And death and disillusion."

"You, turning pessimist, *Padre mio*! This will never do. You are too serious—far too serious. I prescribe a course of Anthony Hope immediately. I have the 'Dolly Dialogues' with me, and you must force yourself to appreciate them. It's plain you have met with little real tragedy in your life, or you would be more cheerful."

"Have you a tragic past, that you are always gay?"

Mary shivered, but she did not answer. She called to Wiggins to come out of the water, for it was growing cold.

The minister scourged himself for four hours afterward, for he noticed that she was pale, and that there were shadows under her brown eyes. What had he said?

VI
MARY'S HUSBAND

Mary had gone to play golf at St. Andrews. The minister called on Mrs. Urquhart anent some parish matters and she detained him, rather against his will, to talk of Mary and her perfections. She never spoke of her except as

"My Miss Mary," and it was apt to bewilder the uninitiated. Suddenly she asked the minister:

"Does she ever talk to you of the wee girlie who was killed?"

"What wee girlie? Never!"

"Eh, it was just an awful thing. Sit down, Mr. Methven, and I'll tell you."

"But, Mrs. Urquhart, do you think if it is so sad, and if she—Mrs. Burton never told me herself—that she would like———"

"Tuts, sir! It's nothing disgraceful; it's just fearfully sad. Ye can only admire her the more for her courage. Well, as I was saying, she had a wee girlie just three years old when they all came home from India on long leave. Master Wiggins was the baby, and Miss Molly was the bonniest creature you ever saw. The Captain—a fine, free-handed gentleman he was, if a wee thing wild—was just wrapped up in her, the boys were nowhere; and he would aye go and fetch her out o' her cot every evening after dinner and play, and nothing Miss Mary could say would stop him. Well, that August they had taken a house down in Cornwall to be near Miss Mary's father. And one evening Miss Mary had gone to dine with an old aunt some miles off, and the Captain and a gentleman staying dined alone. It is thought that the Captain may have taken rather much champagne—he did whiles—but anyway he went and got Miss Molly out of bed and wrapped her in a blanket and carried her out-of-doors. It was no use for the nurse to say anything— he was a masterful gentleman, and brooked no interference. The other gentleman had gone to write letters in the study. Well, Miss Mary came home about ten, and of course went straight up to the night nursery. The little boys were both in bed asleep, but Miss Molly's cot was empty, and the nurse told her the Captain had not brought her up to bed yet. Miss Mary was rather indignant, for she thought it so bad for the child, and went down to fetch her. But the Captain was not in the study, and the other gentleman had not seen him since dinner. He seemed rather alarmed when he heard that Miss Molly was missing, and everybody went out to search the garden, for they were nowhere in the house. They sought and sought, and nothing could they find. Then Miss Mary sent the grooms out with lanterns, and she and the gentleman took the carriage lamps and went down to the foot of the garden where the cliff went sharp down to the sea. There was a steep path cut in the cliff, and down this they went. At the bottom, lying on the hard rock, they found the Captain, with Miss Molly in his arms quite dead, and his back was broken. He lived for three days, and he died with his hand in my dear lady's. She never spoke one word of reproach; but he didn't need it, poor man; his grief was terrible to see, they say. He must have stumbled and fallen sheer over. It's six years ago now; my young lady was only three-and-twenty. Eh, it was a heavy sorrow for a young thing like that!"

Mrs. Urquhart's voice broke, and she stopped. The minister was very white, he held out his hand to her, but did not speak. The Scotch understand each other. They have realized this great truth—that some things are unsayable. The minister held good Mrs. Urquhart's hand in both his for two silent minutes, then he took his hat and went his way.

"He's a grand young man yon!" said Mrs. Urquhart to herself, "he'll make it up till her."

But the young man in question felt that he was further off than ever from his divinity. The wall of unshared experience is high and impassable; we may break it down in places, but it stretches its gaunt length along life's highway and we each of us must keep to our own side.

VII
"BESIDE THE IDLE SUMMER SEA"

"I rather like that minister person," said the Duke to Wiggins in his most patronizing voice, "he seems a decent chap."

"He is," ejaculated Wiggins with immense conviction; "he's a splendid chap—a bit Scotchy, you know, but he's awfully kind."

"The mater likes him too, doesn't she?"

"Oh, yes. He's always with us, you see, living next door and that. He knows all the best places to fish, and he can build the most splendid castles with moats and secret passages and no end!"

The Duke turned his handsome head and smiled indulgently at Wiggins. "I bet he can't shoot or play cricket much, or ride anything but a bike. You can't remember father, Wiggins; he was a soldier, you know, and he used to say: 'Ride straight, shoot straight, and speak the truth, and you'll be a gentleman, sonny.' An officer and a gentleman. I remember though it's so long ago."

The Duke's eyes grew soft. He had loved that big handsome father of his with the uncomprehending, admiring love of a little-noticed child. The little daughter had been everything to Captain Burton, yet the Duke cherished his memory and rendered him a devotion greater than that he gave to the mother who understood him; a devotion which Mary took care should never be disturbed by any word of hers.

As Captain Burton lay dying he had lifted his weak arms and dragged her head down close to his face.

"Don't tell the boys," he whispered. "Let them think the best of me. Duke is a fine chap; he'll make it up to you. I've been a beast and a fool, but I always loved you, Mary. Promise you won't tell the boys."

And Mary promised.

The Duke was a singularly handsome boy, with grave, beautiful manners. He never looked untidy or slovenly. Like his mother, he wore his clothes in such a way that he always seemed better and more suitably dressed than other people. He was rather a silent person, but gave one the impression that he was silent from choice, not because he had nothing to say.

He was very unmistakably a member of the "classes," and though exceedingly urbane and gracious to what he was pleased to call mentally his "inferiors," he was so because it would be ungentlemanly to be otherwise.

He would gravely assist a fishwife to raise her heavy creel to her shoulders, and lift his cap to her with a Hyde Park flourish when she started on her way. But he did so because he considered it the duty of a gentleman to assist women—not as Wiggins would have done, from a friendly interest in that particular fishwife. Slim, tall, and aristocratic, with oval face, straight nose, and big brown eyes, the Duke was a noticeable boy anywhere, and Mary was immensely proud of him.

He was good at most games, and quick to learn. He ferreted out a pony in the next village and rode about the country, to the admiration of the natives. He golfed on the gentlemen's links and played a very good game for his age. He went fishing with the minister and Wiggins, and he bicycled with his mother.

Since the advent of her eldest boy, it seemed to the minister that there was a certain remoteness about Mary. Certainly her time was very much taken up. The Duke required other amusements than those afforded by the beach, a bucket, and a wooden spade. He expected and received the constant companionship of his mother. On several occasions the minister was allowed to join their bicycling expeditions. To watch Mary bicycle was a never-ending wonder to him. She never seemed to go fast; it was only when you rode after her that you found she was hard to catch. The minister always wondered why her skirts never seemed to bunch and blow as did those of other women. He knew nothing of tailors as a great artistic power, but he was keenly alive to the result of their labors in the grace and symmetry of her appearance.

The Duke also was a constant surprise, but for him the minister's frank admiration was tempered by a subtle but searching discomfort in his society.

"Do you know," he said ruefully one day to Mary, "that the Duke makes me conscious of my boots, and the lack of trees to keep them on? I never thought of it before, but I am sure now that it has been a serious omission."

"The Duke is the descendant of generations of dandies, and has all the faults and the good qualities that belong to the class. In many respects the dandy is a limited person both for good and evil; certain social solecisms are, of course, impossible to him, but he generally is lacking in imagination. The Duke, for instance, is less sympathetic than Wiggins, but he is harder on himself also."

"Can a woman be a dandy?" inquired the minister in a tone of grave interest.

Mary laughed. "Every woman of the world is more or less a dandy, but she takes the position less seriously than does a man. If in some directions our sense of proportion is undeveloped, it has arrived at perfection in matters of clothes."

"I'm glad I can only wear one sort of clothes; it saves so much trouble, and I should be certain to get the wrong ones."

"I think you would. Be thankful for your uniform; it is becoming!"

"It's very hot and uncomfortable in summer. I almost feel I could echo Wiggins in his abuse of clothing."

"Why don't you wear flannels?"

"I do for tennis, but one can't call on one's parishioners in flannels; they'd think it casual and disrespectful."

"So they would. Well, you must dree your weird!" Mary spoke lightly, but for the minister her last words had an ominous sound.

Presently they all halted "to give the bicycles a feed" as the Duke put it—the fact being that they had arrived at the foot of what was for Fife a very steep hill. The day was hot, and they had six more miles to do before they reached the East Neuk, whither they were escorting the Duke. Grass and the shade of trees looked inviting. Mary and the minister decided to rest, but the energetic Duke went off on an exploring expedition in an adjacent wood.

The minister and Mary sat quite silent for some minutes; then Mary said slowly:

"Mrs. Urquhart told you of my great trouble six years ago. I am glad. I wanted you to know, and I wanted you to know that I am glad." Her voice was very soft, her eyes were bent on the grass.

Andrew Methven looked at her but he did not speak.

She looked up a little surprised, and saw his face working strangely. She understood.

"Don't try to say anything," she said, laying her hand on his arm. "You are sorry. You are a good friend of mine."

Somehow the touch of the little gloved hand on his arm made the minister lose his head. He did not attempt to hold it in his own—his reverence for her was too great for that—but he told her simply and forcibly what he felt for her. She did not try to stop him. The sunshine and the summer had got into her blood, and this worship that was offered to her was sweet and precious. There was nothing ridiculous in it, nothing impossible. He did not ask her to be his wife; in his wildest dreams of happiness he had never reckoned on the possibility of that. He did not ask to be anything to her; all he told her was what she was to him.

And in the very middle of it all the Duke came back, saying:

"If we are to get to the East Neuk by teatime, we'd better be off; it's four already."

So they rode off, and very silent companions the Duke found them.

Seven years before in Simla, Mary had had a great success. She had been made much of, and had enjoyed it. Many men had made love to her, and she had enjoyed it. A beautiful, healthy girl accepts admiration as her natural right.

But the men who made love to her did not enjoy it, for many of them had the misfortune to be serious, and although Mary accepted their flowers and their compliments and their devotion in her own gay, gracious fashion, she gave nothing in return but that gay graciousness and the privilege of her society.

"If she were in love with that card-playing, drinking fool, her husband, I could understand it," said Major Molyneux of the 42nd; "but she isn't in love with him, not a bit; and yet she's an icicle to every other chap. It's not as if she were one of those cold, saint-in-a-shrine sort of women; she's as human as she can be. She's no fool, either. What, in heaven's name, made her marry her husband?"

"Calm yourself, my dear Molly! Calm yourself," answered the elderly civilian to whom he was unburdening himself. "You have yet to learn that the selective faculty is latest of development in women. Most women, especially if they are pretty, marry before it has developed at all. If they are good as well as pretty, they take care it shan't develop afterwards."

"Burton hasn't even the grace to be jealous; he lets her do just what she pleases. He's so mighty conceited that he never seems to think she may come across a man capable of understanding her."

The commissioner smiled. "I don't think much of Burton's intellectual capacity, but I do give him credit for this—he understands his wife, and because he understands her, he trusts her absolutely. It's no use, my dear boy, Simla will never have the pleasure of discussing Mrs. Burton in connection with any sort of scandal; she's not that kind!"

The commissioner was right. Her husband never had reason to find fault with Mary, and since his death she had devoted herself to her boys and to the cultivation of her mind. She took it as a matter of course that men should fall in love with her; they always did. But her experience did not make her eager to investigate further the realms of marriage.

Men made love to her because they wanted to possess her. She was so tired of hearing, "Don't you understand? I want you for myself, for my very own."

Mary understood, but as yet she had felt no desire to belong to anybody in that exclusive fashion.

Andrew Methven touched her. Here at last was the Princely Giver she had dreamed of, as women will dream, the man ready to give everything, asking only for leave to lay his homage at her feet, nothing more.

When she had first met him, she set him down as one of those who are destined "to do something." It was not his fate to remain an obscure Free Kirk minister, of that she was sure. The more she saw of him the more she felt the reality of the strange power that lay behind his apparently commonplace views of men and things. "It is there," she said to herself exultingly, and now that he had made love to her in this strange, unusual way, she was seized with a passionate desire to take this man into her life, and help him to give form and substance to that latent force of his.

So Mary dreamed dreams while she listened to the minister as he discoursed upon the historical interests of the East Neuk; as they rode home swiftly and for the most part silently; as, the Duke having gone to bed, she sat at the open window and watched the moonlight on the sea.

Then she went and looked at the boys in their two little straight beds side by side. As she bent over the Duke he smiled, and threw his arm round her neck, murmuring sleepily, "Dear mater."

Shading the candle with her hand, she looked long and greedily at the sleeping children, and, like all women at such moments, the triumphant sense of possession swamped every other feeling.

As she reached her own room and stood before her glass, she looked into the reflected eyes, saying: "Take ship, for happiness is somewhere to be had!"

VIII
THE COLONEL INTERFERES

"There's little Burton. I'll ask him if it's true," ejaculated Colonel Colquhoun, as he noticed three or four small red-coated figures coming down the long slope at the far end of the gentlemen's links.

"No, not the child; I would not ask the child if I were you, Colquhoun." Mr. Braid spoke earnestly, laying his hand on the colonel's arm to detain him. "He may know nothing about it, you know, there may be nothing to know. In any case I wouldn't ask the boy."

But Colonel Colquhoun had just made an inferior drive, he was in a bad temper as are many people during the royal and ancient game, so he bustled off, ignoring his friend's remonstrance, toward the putting-green where the Duke was triumphantly holing in after a specially brilliant placing of his ball.

The caddie shouldered the colonel's clubs, and Mr. Braid followed more slowly. He felt a curious disinclination to join the little group on the putting-green. His own lad—just home from Fettes—was one of the players; he had said kind things of the pluck and perseverance of little Burton. Mr. Braid's heart was tender, and he himself had not forgotten the moment when he first heard of a possible stepfather. He walked more and more slowly.

The hole that the Duke and his friends were playing was the last on the links; the boyish figures were outlined sharply against the sky. Mr. Braid saw the Duke lift his cap as the colonel came up. He could not hear what passed, but he saw the four boys turn, and one after another tee their balls and drive. The colonel was left alone on the putting-green, where his ball was not. The caddie stood grinning, and the colonel cuffed his ears, declaring that the young ruffian had stolen his ball.

Mr. Braid waited in patience till the ball was discovered in some distant bents, but the colonel did not again mention little Burton or his mother.

The Duke was playing abominably. Halfway home he said: "Braid, would you think me an awful cad if I break up the foursome? I can't play a hang." The child's lips were quivering, and his sunburnt cheeks looked white under the tan.

Braid put his arm round his shoulders affectionately. "You go home, old chap. You're hipped, but never mind that old beast Colquhoun, he's always making mischief. Don't you notice him."

"I didn't—much, did I?" the Duke asked anxiously. "I hope I didn't—show."

"Not you—not a bit. Here, scoot! I'll bring your clubs."

The Duke broke into a run, and regardless of the enraged "fores" which sounded on every side, made straight across the links to the rocky shore. There he would be alone—alone with this terrible possibility that flashed its lurid light across his path.

Once behind the rocks he sat down and sobbed, even as he did so wondering when he had cried before. The Duke did not "blub"—never—he considered tears unworthy of a man, "of an officer and a gentleman," had not the father whose memory he adored once said to him: "Curse if you like, old man, but never cry." So the Duke never cried, though his language on occasions would have surprised his mother by its forcible variety. Before ladies, though, "gentlemen do not swear," so Mary remained in blissful ignorance of her son's proficiency in certain forms of objurgation.

Now, however, the Duke sobbed, great tearing, dreadful sobs that racked his slender body with a pain that was almost physical.

The colonel had done his work. As he walked across the green to enlighten Duke, he had said to himself: "I'll make it hot for Mrs. Burton, haughty minx; the boy's a tartar."

Mary had found it necessary to snub the colonel on more than one occasion; so he no longer called her "a monstrous fine woman." A fancied slight rankles in the mean and narrow soul; revenge is doubly sweet if one near and dear to the offender can be made the instrument of punishment.

The Duke sat behind the rocks and sobbed until he felt sick and stupid. Had he not heard of that horrible institution called a stepfather? Had he not read only last holidays a book called "David Copperfield," wherein the iniquities of such an one were set forth with terrible distinctness.

He was not a religious child. Mary was not dogmatic in her teaching, she influenced more by her example and her mental attitude than by conscious effort. Yet here and now the boy felt that circumstances were too strong for him, and he prayed in a hopeless, muddled fashion that if his mother did this thing, God would take him to join the father she seemed to have forgotten.

It is a mistake to think that children never come face to face with despair. They do, more often than the superior, omniscient grown-ups themselves. There is a finality about every sorrow for children, they cannot realize that such pain as they feel *can* pass; they do not believe it. That saddest of all poets must have thought of sorrowing children when he wrote:

We are most hopeless, who had once most hope,

And most beliefless, who had most believed.

What matter if the grief be short, its poignancy while it lasts is none the less acute.

The Duke stopped crying, and looked at the bare wall of rock before him with hopeless, unseeing eyes. Then as he prayed, a great wave of tenderness, of longing for his mother, broke over his child soul, and he got up. Scrambling over the great boulder he had hidden behind, he set off to run home. If this amazing, this shameful news were true, he would set a seal on his misery, and uncertainty would be at an end. If it were false, the Duke set his teeth as he thought of the colonel, then he squared his shoulders and dropped into the swinging run which made him such an admirable hare at "hare and hounds."

He ran by the beach, a good three miles, and burst into their little sitting-room, tear-stained and breathless, just as Mary had arranged her writing-board on her knee.

She looked up in astonishment at his somewhat noisy entrance. He still wore his cap in the room, before her, and his face was dirty. Who had seen the Duke with a dirty face since he arrived at years of discretion?

"My darling boy, what has happened? Is it Wiggins? Is he hurt?" Mary stood up in her excitement, and the paper and envelopes were scattered about the floor.

The Duke only looked at her, his lips trembling.

"Speak, Duke, what is it? Don't keep me in suspense."

"No one is hurt, mother, except me, and I'm only hurt in my heart." The tears ran down his cheeks as he spoke. "Mother, is it true—are you going to marry Mr. Methven? Oh, say it isn't true. It's so dreadful!"

Mary drew the boy to her, and sitting down she took him on her knee. He buried his dirty face in her neck and sobbed.

"My dearest, who has said that I am going to marry Mr. Methven? Surely you do not suspect me of telling people—other people—before I would tell you such a thing as that! Oh, Duke, I thought you trusted me."

"But, mother, you might not have *told* them, they might have guessed, and it's not the not knowing that I mind, it's—it's—Mr. Methven!"

"Dear Duke, did it never strike you as possible that I might marry again?"

"Never! Never! You belong to Wiggins and me—and father. Have you forgotten father?"

"No, sonny, no. I have not forgotten."

"Oh, mother, say it isn't true, say it isn't true, or I shall die!"

Mary folded the boy closer in her arms. "It is not true, dear. Mr. Methven has not even asked me to marry him."

As she spoke she remembered her own words as she looked into the glass the night before. Her face grew very sad.

"But if he did ask you, mother, you would say no? You would say no?"

The Duke's voice, husky with long crying, was very pathetic.

Mary leaned back in her chair and closed her eyes. She held her boy very close, and her breath came quickly.

"I don't think he will ask me, dear, but if he does, I must say no, for his sake!"

The Duke sat up and gazed at his mother in absolute amazement.

"For his sake," he repeated in a hushed, almost frightened voice. "Do you want to marry him, mother?"

"It does not matter much what I want to do, my little son; it's what I must *not* do that we have to do with. I shall not marry Mr. Methven. Some day when you are a man you will realize what I have given up for you—and for him!" And Mary fell a-weeping with her boy clasped in her arms.

The Duke felt her hot tears on his short-cropped hair, and he trembled; then, releasing himself from his mother's arms, got off her knee and stood beside her, very pale and grave.

"Dear!" he said solemnly, "if you want to marry this—gentleman—if it will make you happier, you shall. Do you hear, darling? You shall." And throwing himself into his mother's arms, they cried together. When it came to the point, he found that he loved his mother better—than himself.

Presently Mary began to laugh. "Oh, Duke, Duke, how funny you are! You talk as if I were a little girl, as if—but it doesn't matter—some day you will understand.... It's not going to happen, Duke dear. It's been a storm in a teacup. You must never listen to what ignorant people say."

"May I contradict them, politely?" asked the Duke eagerly, with an immense relief shining in his eyes.

"Certainly, if anyone has the impertinence to speak of such a thing again. It is an insult to Mr. Methven and to me. Oh, Duke, there's somebody coming upstairs. Quick, go and say I've got a headache and can't see people."

It flashed across the boy's mind that he was not very presentable either. However, the staircase was dark, and he shut the sitting-room door behind him. A tall, black-coated figure was ascending the stairs.

"Mother can't see anyone to-day, Mr. Methven; she's got a headache."

But even as he spoke the door at the top of the stairs opened, and Mary said:

"I'll see Mr. Methven, sonny, but ask Mrs. Urquhart to say I am engaged if anyone else calls."

The sitting-room door closed behind the minister and Mary. The Duke went to his own room to wash his face, and to ponder over his mother's words.

IX
VALE

Somebody has said that women have no sense of humor. It is one of those knock-me-down assertions that provoke argument. The sense of humor is so blessed a gift, it were unjust indeed to deny its benefits to the larger half of humanity. The gods had bestowed it with no niggardly hand upon Mary. It had stood her in good stead during many a crisis; its divine attribute did not desert her now.

There was a poetic justice in the appearance of Andrew Methven at that particular moment that appealed to her sense of artistic inevitability; and as Andrew shut the door behind him, though the tears shone wet upon her cheeks, she laughed.

"I am sorry you have a headache," began Andrew lamely. "Shall I go away?"

"No, sit down; I want to talk to you. I've just been through a somewhat trying scene with the Duke, and I long that somebody should horsewhip Colonel Colquhoun."

"I don't possess a horsewhip, but I have a good stout stick." The minister's manner was most unclerical as his grasp tightened on the weapon in question.

"You do not even ask what he has done."

"He has annoyed you—that is quite enough; but I wish he was a younger man."

"He is not young enough to thrash, and he is not quite old enough to ignore; all the same, we shall have to ignore him. But, you Quixotic person, would you really thrash a man because I asked you to?"

"If you asked me to thrash a man, I should know he well deserved thrashing, and I—should enjoy it."

"You're more man than minister, after all," said Mary, more to herself than to him.

"Better man, better minister. Do you think I could have had any sort of influence over my colliers at Cowdenbeath if I couldn't fight? I can't fence, but I can box. I'll teach the Duke, if you like."

"Why don't you ask me what Colonel Colquhoun has done?"

"Because if you want to tell me, you will tell me; and if it is unpleasant to you to tell me, why should you?"

"It's as unpleasant as it is necessary I should tell you, because we must both publicly contradict a foolish report that has got spread abroad in Elgo to the effect that we are to be married."

Mary did not blush as she spoke, but the minister crimsoned to the roots of his hair. "I am too sorry you should have been subjected to this annoyance. You know what my feeling for you is; you also know that I have not the right to ask a fisher lass to marry me. I am nothing, and have nothing; but you have let me lay my great love at your feet."

Mary made a little sound, half sob, half laugh, and held out her hands to him in a helpless, unseeing way that went to his heart. He caught them in his own, and looking into the dear face with purple shadows painted by tears under the eyes, he knew that she, too, cared.

What does it avail to tell in words how these two plighted their troth, that was to be ever unfulfilled? The tenderest and truest of lovers have generally small literary value.

For half an hour they went to heaven together.

Then they faced realities, and Andrew asked: "Will you write to me?"

Mary shook her head. "No; if we write we shall simply waste our lives in everlasting watching for the postman. We are very human, you and I, and how can we hope to be better and wiser than other people?"

"You are hard," murmured Andrew. "I can find no comfort in virtuous soliloquy. A letter would be something tangible."

"No, I am not hard; but I am old who once was young, and I know. As it is we shall have a perfect and unspoiled memory, full of tenderness and grace and poetry; but if we write we shall be miserable, ever unsatisfied, hanging, like Mahomet's coffin, between heaven and earth. No; let us keep this sweet experience untarnished by impotent tears and regrets."

Three days after, Mary and her boys had joined some of the numerous uncles at a shooting-box near Kingussie. The Duke was very happy; but Wiggins missed his beloved sea. "I think my minister must miss me," he said. "I miss him so very much; he's such a kind man."

PART III
CHILDREN OF THIS

JEAN, A PORTRAIT

She was remarkable in the first place because she never rode in a perambulator like other children; either she walked—on bare, shapely, pink feet—or her own personal attendant, Elspeth (a very tall woman indeed), carried her in a plaid slung over one of her broad shoulders. Elspeth despised the "bit barrows" of the other nurses, and was quite strong enough to have carried Jean's mother as well as Jean. "She will go barefoot," Elspeth would say, "till she iss seven, and when she iss a woman she will walk like a queen, and not like a hen!"

Jean, if possible, went bareheaded as well as "barefoot," and perhaps that is the reason why her hair is so abundant, so curly, so full of golden light that in the sunshine it almost makes you blink. Moreover, her eyes are big and blue. Sunshine and rain, and kind fresh winds have tinted her face with the loveliest warm browns and pinks; she is not yet five years old, and she can dance the sword dance! It is really a great sight to see Jean's pink feet twinkling in and out between two unsheathed swords of her father's, and he is a proud man.

Yet there never was such a "girly" girl as Jean.

She has an enormous family of dolls—for her adorers all bring dolls, and *they* are as the sands of the sea in number—she takes a motherly interest in them all, both dolls and adorers, but her inseparable companion is one "Tammy," an ancient and dirty-faced rag soldier; with arms and legs resembling elongated sausages, a square body, no feet, and a head shaped like a breakfast "bap." Not an attractive personality to the uninitiated, but he and Jean were as Ruth and Naomi. It is something of a sorrow to her that the exigencies of Tammy's figure do not admit of a kilt, just as she puzzled all last summer in sorrowful surprise that her father never once donned the uniform she so admires.

Jean's people live at a house on the Terrace, which has at the back a shady old-fashioned garden with a big square lawn in the centre. There Jean's brothers, Colin and Andrew, played cricket, while Jean fielded or drilled her dolls under the trees. In the evening, after dinner, there would be a sound of men's voices and an occasional thrum of the banjo under those same trees, and a cheerful clink of glasses, while men with brown faces and trim, well-set heads laughed and rejoiced in a coolness that concealed no malaria.

Jean's father had a reprehensible habit of bringing her, wrapped in a blanket, out into the garden at ten o'clock at night, when she would be handed about from knee to knee like a superior sort of refreshment. To be fetched out of bed in this fashion would have been upsetting to some children, but Jean, with an adorable sleepy smile, would make herself agreeable for half an hour or so, and when carried back and tucked into bed—always by her father—fell asleep again directly, and never seemed a scrap the worse. On such occasions she was always expected to sing. She never sang anything but Scottish songs—mournful or martial, mostly Jacobite, and her repertory was enormous. While other children were learning "Little Jack Horner," or "Hey diddle diddle!" Jean, thanks to Elspeth, learned "Hey Johnny Cope," or "Cam' ye by Athol," and her voice was as the voice of Katherine of France, "broken music," for her voice was music, and her English broken. Sometimes a belated passer-by would wait outside to listen in wonder to someone singing in the clearest baby voice:

Sing Hey, my bra' John Hielandman,

Sing Ho, my bra' John Hielandman,

and at the end of each refrain she always kissed her father, for there was no one in the world to match with him in Jean's eyes. She absolutely declined to sing the last verse after that day upon which she discovered what "hanging" meant, Colin and Andrew having suspended Tammy from the apple tree. At times, Jean could raise her voice otherwise than in song, and on that occasion the whole Terrace resounded with her shrieks.

Next door there dwelt a very grumpy gentleman. With that easy confidence in a neighbor's neighborliness generally manifested by people who have lived much abroad, Jean's father, on taking up his quarters, had written asking permission to put some wire-netting on the top of the party wall to prevent cricket balls going over. To his immense surprise he received a curt and discourteous refusal, which terminated in a warning to the effect that, if balls did come over, there they would have to stay, as the writer would in no circumstances have boys running in and out of his house, and there was no back entrance. Of course balls went over; but Colin and Andrew found an unexpected ally in Mr. Knagg's housekeeper, who threw the balls back again without consulting him; and Mr. Knagg felt rather aggrieved that, as yet, he had found no cause for complaint. Complaint in some form or other was as the breath of life to him; he had gone to law with so many of his fellow-townsmen that his society was no longer sought after, and his exceedingly clean steps were untrodden by strangers. He intended at first to complain that the banjo-playing in the garden disturbed him at his studies, when he happened to hear Jean sing "This iss no my plaid," and somehow he gave up the idea.

Colin and Andrew possessed a "mashie" each, and a game of "putting golf." It was reserved for Sunday afternoons as being of a quiet and decorous nature.

But one Sunday afternoon Andrew forgot to "putt," and gave his ball a drive that lifted it high over the wall into the next garden. Now, the wall was too high to climb; besides, the fear of Mr. Knagg was upon them, and the housekeeper was out—they had seen her go. They had only two balls, and it was yet a long two hours off teatime. Father and mother were both out. They retired to consult Jean under the trees.

"If he wasn't such an old beast, I'd go and ask for it myself," growled Andrew.

"You wouldn't get it if you did," said Colin the practical.

"Why shouldn't Jean go? He'd give it to her," suggested Andrew, who had noted the weakness of his sex where Jean was concerned.

"Of course he would. You must go, Jean. Hurry up!"

"What, all on my lonely?" exclaimed Jean in pained astonishment.

"Oh, we'll come with you to the door and ring the bell for you, and then cut away before he can open it. Then you ask him nicely. Come on, Jean!"

She seldom long opposed her brothers. She had what Elspeth called a "tender head," and strongly objected to having her hair pulled. Between them they marched her up the flagged path to Mr. Knagg's front door, rang loudly, and departed precipitately.

Maighda, the great deerhound who shared with Elspeth the guardianship of Jean, rose from amidst the company of dolls, where she had been reposing, and walking gravely into the front garden, jumped the iron fence, and joined Jean at the top of the steps.

Jean clasped Tammy firmly with one arm and coiled the other round Maighda's neck as the door opened rather noisily to disclose an irate-looking little gentleman in gold-rimmed *pince-nez*.

"If you please," began Jean, in a still, small voice, "there iss a wee ball-y wass putted into your garden—will I get it?"

Mr. Knagg stood staring at his strange visitors, while Jean rubbed one pink foot over the other and Maighda sniffed at him dubiously. Tammy, with his customary reserve, betrayed no emotion whatever.

"Come!" said Mr. Knagg shortly, holding out his hand. As Jean disappeared Colin and Andrew flew into the back garden and swarmed up an apple tree, whence they surveyed their sister's proceedings with interest.

"Wonder why men are so much decenter to girls than to us?" mused Andrew.

"Oh, well; his housekeeper likes us best, anyway. Everyone's got their cranks."

"Fore," cried a clear little voice, and the ball fell with a soft "plop" at the foot of the apple tree.

"She throws very well for a girl," said Colin as he dropped onto the grass. "Let's finish the game."

"What do you mean by 'fore'?" asked Mr. Knagg.

"Heads, you know," said Jean; but her host was more puzzled than ever, for he had not even a bowing acquaintance with the royal and ancient game. They stared at each other in silence for a minute, then Jean, remembering that one of the most important precepts of her clan was to accept no service without rendering some return, said shyly: "Will I sing you a song?"

"Pray do!" exclaimed Mr. Knagg; and his eyeglasses flew off his nose, he frowned so hard.

"My love's in Germanie—send him hame! send him hame! My love's in Germanie—send him hame!" Jean only sang three verses. Elspeth never taught her the last two, and when the last notes full of longing had died away, she added cheerfully: "But he iss at home just now."

"Who is?"

"My father. Nearly all my songs iss about father."

"Really!" ejaculated Mr. Knagg, and blew his nose noisily. "So that's Scotch?"

"All my songs iss Scottish. I promised Elspeth, and I will know them all some day. Goot-bye!" and Jean, settling Tammy more comfortably on her arm, prepared to depart. As she spoke she had lifted her face to be kissed, and Mr. Knagg kissed her.

"He iss a dull man," said Jean confidentially to Colin; "but he was douce enough to me."

The man in question sat in his favorite chair and read his Sunday newspaper upside down. It was thirty-five years since he had kissed a child!

Colin and Andrew were at school, father and mother had gone out in the dog-cart, taking Maighda with them for the run, Elspeth was ironing frocks, and Jean entertaining Tammy and all the dolls at tea on the lawn. Suddenly she threw back her head and listened—no one had such quick ears as Jean— the color rushed to her face, and she scampered across the grass, round by the side of the house, and out at the garden gate; bareheaded, with flying rosy feet, she raced to the end of the terrace, and as she ran the sound which so excited her grew louder. It was the pipes!

Would she find "the regiment," she wondered? Had it come to show what Elspeth called "this wee stuck-up bit towney" what real John Hielandman were like? Jean pictured the frowning castle and windy Esplanade, the steep, stony street, flanked by tall grey houses, down which "the regiment" "in tartan plaid and philabeg" swept with swinging steps. That was the setting in which she knew her father's men. How would they look in this trim Southern town? And would she dare to stop them to ask after her friends?

No, it was not a march the piper was playing, and very soon she discovered that there was no regiment—only a solitary piper playing the "Keel Row," with a crowd of unkempt children following him.

Jean pushed in among the children, who made way for this hatless, shoeless person in some astonishment.

"He iss not the 'Forty-second,' nor the 'Gordons,' nor the 'Seaforth,'" said Jean to herself, "and why will he wear two tartans?" Then, pulling at the piper's kilt, she cried shrilly, above the skirl of the pipes: "Can you play 'Oran an Aoig'?"

The piper took the chanter out of his mouth, and smiled down at the eager, upturned face, asking: "*Wot*, my dear?"

"'Oran an Aoig,'" repeated Jean eagerly.

"Sorry I cawn't oblige you, but I never 'eard tell of that toon," and the "Keel Row" sounded with renewed and aggressive vigor.

Jean loosed her hold of the kilt and turned to go. There was something uncanny in the speech of this piper, and as she looked more closely, a certain incongruity in his uniform which chilled and disappointed her. The children, however, having recovered from their surprise at her sudden appearance in their midst, decided to have some fun with Jean, and she speedily discovered that to be the only shoeless person in a heavily shod crowd is to be in a most unpleasant minority. Also, she had never been alone in the street before.

Mr. Knagg heard the pipes on his way home to lunch, and having the greatest abhorrence of all street noises, holding that they were, every one, "disturbing to the peace of His Majesty's lieges," was hurrying across the road to expostulate with the perpetrator of this new outrage upon his ears, when he caught sight of a familiar shining in the very middle of that rabble of children. He laid about him with his white cotton umbrella, presently emerged from the crowd, bearing a very tearful Jean in his arms, and hailed a cab. The cab and the dog-cart drove up to Jean's door at the same moment. Mr. Knagg left Jean on the pavement and stalked into his house.

"I said he was a douce man," sobbed Jean, in the safe shelter of her father's arms; "but it wass a pittence piper, not one of ours at all." They say that she felt the deception even more than the bruises on her toes. Her father never managed to thank Mr. Knagg though he called three times.

"Of course the master's gone to the war with the regiment. He only got six months' leave, after all, and Miss Jean talks and sings about him all day long, and the mistress just listens. But she says if Master Colin and Master Andrew were older, she'd send them, too; for there's aye been some of our family for the men to follow." Elspeth left Mr. Knagg's housekeeper standing at the wire fence, for she "never encouraged clash."

In the wintry days her neighbors saw less of Jean, as play in the garden was impossible. But even then the pink feet splashed bravely through the puddles and over the wet stones.

One evening about six, just as Mr. Knagg was turning into the Terrace, a newspaper boy, shouting with raucous voice, proclaimed: "Serious British Reverse!" "'Ighland regiment trapped and cut to pieces!" The old gentleman darted across the road, crying: "Stop that infernal din, and I'll buy every rag you've got! Don't come down here again, mind!"

He hurried down the Terrace with a great bundle of pink papers under his arm. Just outside his own house he paused and looked up. Jean's nursery window was open at the top, the curtains were not drawn, and the room was full of rosy light. Suddenly a child's voice soared into the stillness:

He's as brave as brave can be;

Send him hame, send him hame!

He's as brave as brave can be;

Send him hame!

Mr. Knagg took off his hat and bent his head.

THE DOLL'S-HOUSE FLAGS (1917)

To begin with the youngest.

"Me an' the war's the same age," said Jasper, for Jasper was born on August 4th, 1914.

Perhaps that was why he manifested such a decided and independent disposition almost from his earliest months.

It may have been that everybody was so busy he was more thrown upon his own resources than are babies in more leisurely times. But whatever the reason, he ran about when he was one, talked fluently—if in somewhat impressionistic fashion—when he was eighteen months old, and by the time he was two he had attained very definite characteristics.

Barbara came next, four long years older than Jasper. She had a round, rosy face and kind brown eyes that readily filled with tears, and her little heart overflowed with love and pity for the wounded.

Alison was quite old when war broke out. She could remember times when sweets "were nothing so very much—everybody eat them," when "gentlemen often had *two* eggs for breakfast and lots of other things as well," when "Mummy could buy anything she liked in shops, and nearly everybody had motors."

Alison was six when Jasper was born.

Tall and pale was Alison, with straight black hair that reached her waist. She took the war very seriously indeed, and was implacable in her conviction that nothing else mattered. She was even rather shocked that mummy could take comfort in the thought that it would probably be over before Jasper was old enough to join up.

Then there was George.

He was an American and the same age as Alison and lived quite near, though after the unfriendly fashion of London, they might never have known him but that it happened his mummy and theirs worked at the same hospital.

He was an "only," and when they first knew him went as a day boy to a preparatory school quite a long way off; but as time went on and transport of every kind became more crowded and difficult, he came to do lessons with Alison and Barbara.

Nothing made Barbara so happy as to be allowed to visit the "dear poor ones" in the hospital where mummy worked; but when she first saw the blind soldiers from St. Dunstan's and they were explained to her, it seemed as though she really could not bear the knowledge. The children lived on the south side of Regent's Park, and Nannie always took them there for their walks.

"Will they never be able to see?" she would ask piteously.

"I fear not in this life," was Nannie's invariable answer.

"Not anything? Ever?"

"Nothing at all. But they are very brave, Miss Barbara; *they* don't cry."

For days after when Barbara met them in Regent's Park, her mouth would go down at the corners, and though she did not actually cry she was, as nurse said, "queer and quiet" for a long time afterward. Their inexorable doom weighed on her little soul, and even her serene faith in a kind God and protecting angels and the "tender Shepherd" of her prayers was somewhat shaken that such a cruel thing could be. Ah! if they could only have met *Him*! He would have "touched their eyes" and all would have been well. Perhaps some day—— In the meantime the fairies—and she believed in them as firmly as in the heavenly hierarchy itself—came to her aid, and by some process of reasoning she decided that the blinded soldiers were under an enchantment. That a wicked ogre, a German ogre, had taken away their sight (even as trolls and cruel step-mothers and evilly disposed fairies blinded her favorite heroes in the "Tales from the Norse"), but that some day a kind fairy or wise, friendly beast would put them in the way of getting their eyes back again. Surely among all the animals in the Zoo there would be one who knew exactly under what tree in the Park the healing dew might be found.

She never spoke of the St. Dunstan's men as blind, but as the "poor enchanted ones," to distinguish them from the "dear poor ones" of the hospital, and she would never speak of "Blindman's Buff," but always of "Enchanted Buff."

Jasper had learned to salute and was immensely proud of himself. Every man in khaki or hospital blue that came in his way, from brass-hats to the most newly joined recruits, received his respectful and ecstatic salutation. Two-foot-six in a white Persian lamb coat and white gaiters would stand rigidly to attention and bring up a diminutive hand clad in a white glove smartly to his forehead. If the man he desired to honor happened to be in hospital blue, he then kissed his hand to express affection as well as respect. When the warrior in question perceived Jasper he invariably returned the courtesy with *empressement*. Generals were most punctilious in this matter, and when Jasper saw one coming he would trot forward, plant himself firmly in the line of vision of the eyes under the brass hat, and, rosy and triumphant, wait till Nannie came up, announcing proudly: "I t'luted 'im *and* he t'luted me."

Everyone smiled upon Jasper. He was so small and round and earnest, and his absurd hair curled around the edge of his cap in the most entrancing fashion. He knew he was popular and enjoyed it amazingly.

Therefore was he surprised and chilled when one day, having as usual trotted ahead of Nannie, he stopped opposite two blue soldiers resting on a seat in the park and they took not the slightest notice of him.

They seemed to be looking right at him as he stood at salute, but they neither "t'luted," nor did they smile or speak.

Jasper kissed his hand.

Still no response.

He kissed his hand, and blew the kiss right at them.

Puzzled, he looked from one to the other. They weren't asleep. Their eyes were wide open, and their faces kind and patient, but they didn't seem a bit glad to see him.

They just took no notice—no notice at all. And Nannie came up with the pram.

"I t'luted 'em," he said in rather trembling tones, quite unlike his usual strong treble, "but they don't seem to like me."

"Eh, what?" said one of the men suddenly. "What's that?"

Nannie said something hurriedly in a low voice. "He's only two and a bit," she added. Then, "It's too cold for you to be sitting there. Have you lost your bearings?"

"That's about it," said the man who had first spoken. "Perhaps you'll put us on our way. It's time we were getting back."

"We'll go with you. Give him your hand, dear, and bring him along."

"I *did* t'lute 'em," Jasper said again, feeling that an important ceremony had somehow been scamped.

Both the men stood up, and the one who had spoken to Nannie jogged his friend with his elbow, saying: "And so do we salute you, young man," and they both did.

The man put down his hand and touched the top of Jasper's Persian lamb cap, and laughed:

"What a big man!" he said.

And hand in hand they followed Nannie to St. Dunstan's.

"Now you know what it's like for the poor enchanted ones," Barbara said, taking her hands from Jasper's eyes.

Jasper looked very solemn. "Poor 'chanted ones," he echoed; "I'll t'lute 'em and kiss my hand *and* kirtsey ne'st time I meet 'em."

"You talk to them, my dear," said sensible Nannie; "they'll like that better than all your salutin's."

This Jasper was most ready to do at great length in his little high voice that the poor enchanted ones came to recognize a long way off. But all the same he never failed to "t'lute and kiss his hand *and* kirtsey." No signs of respect and affection could be too much, Barbara said.

"It's the worst thing of all, so we must love them most."

Fairies and angels were inextricably mixed up in Barbara's mind, and when her mother came to kiss her good-night on Christmas Eve, she murmured sleepily: "I simply can't 'astinguish between God and Father Christmas, so I mus' just let it alone."

Even the toys were much affected by the war. Jasper's Teddy Bear wore an expression not unlike the pathetic puzzled look of his brethren in the Mappin Circle, now that nobody threw them buns, sat they on their tails never so pleadingly. Alison had made him the brassard of a special constable, and he always wore it when he went out with Jasper in the pram. The lady dolls had all become V.A.D.'s or bus conductors or window-cleaners, and one quite recent acquisition was a land girl.

As for the doll's house, it wore a martial yet festive air, for the flags of all the allies were stuck in a tight band of string with which Alison had bound it thrice just under the roof.

It was not a new doll's house. In fact as doll's houses go it was almost venerable. It had belonged to grannie's mother, and was built in the early part of Queen Victoria's reign. Unlike modern doll's houses, it did not open in front. In front it was square and solid, with two large windows on either side of the door, which had glass panels, and actually opened and shut, and there were three oblong windows on the next floor. The roof was made of real little slates, with chimneys at either end of it. The ground floor was a shop, with two black counters that could be taken out and dusted, and the walls were fitted with innumerable shelves and cupboards. It was a silversmith's shop, and on the brass plates under the windows were, on one, "David Strachan, Silversmith and Jeweler," on the other, "By Appointment to Her Majesty Queen Victoria." By which it could be seen that it was a Scottish jeweler's shop, for nobody called "Strachan" could be of any other nationality. Moreover, there were tiny toddy-ladles of various sizes among the stock-in-trade.

Daddy used to tell the children an entrancing serial story about the inhabitants of this wonderful house, whereof most of the plenishings remained in their original form, though Mr. and Mrs. Strachan, the two shop assistants, and the baby, had been renewed from time to time, but always as nearly as possible resembling their predecessors. Thus it came about that Mr. Strachan had side-whiskers—daddy painted them himself—a stock and peg-top trousers, and Mrs. Strachan a crinoline and an amazingly slender waist; while Jenny, the maid, who slept in a box-bed in the kitchen, had a mob-cap and always wore her sleeves rolled up. The bedroom of Mr. and Mrs. Strachan was much bemuslined, and the parlor had green rep chairs and a round table.

"It's all of our doll's house," Barbara used to say. "It doesn't belong to anyone partickler. Grannie said so."

"George's, too," Jasper always added. He couldn't bear George to be left out of anything.

And perhaps because George was an American he was a little less on his dignity than an English boy of the same age. He didn't despise girls, he treated them in a comradely fashion that Alison and Barbara greatly appreciated. And Jasper adored him, for George realized that a person might be not quite three, with nether garments so abbreviated as to be almost indistinguishable from petticoats, with woolly gaiters and shoes so small they refused to make a martial tramp, however much one tried—and yet the said person might possess the most boyish soul in the world.

Therefore was George made free of the doll's house, and assisted Alison with the serial story which she had taken over since that day, early in the war, when daddy went with his Territorial battalion to France.

It was on New Year's Day in 1917 that George brought Alison the American flag for the doll's house. It was a beautiful little silk one, and he had selected it himself at Selfridge's.

"I'd like Mr. Strachan should have it," he said. "We want the allies to win. You bet we do."

But Alison shook her head. "I'm sorry," she said. "I hate not to take it—I'll have it myself if you like, but it can't go on the house. Not yet it can't. America's not in, you see."

"After all," said George, "we've done a good bit, haven't we? Look at my dad—he's been driving an ambulance—he gave it himself—ever since the beginning of the war, and he's been wounded."

"I know," Alison answered, "I know all that, but"—and her grave little face was set like a flint—"you're not in it yet, you're not *fighting*, and only countries that are fighting *with* us can have their flags on the doll's house. Mr. Strachan's most partickler about that. My daddy's been wounded twice."

"Wouldn't he have it at the back?" Barbara suggested. She couldn't bear people to be hurt, and George looked very much hurt.

"No, thank you," he said haughtily. "If it can't be put with the others, you needn't have it at all. It's a great flag."

"I know," said Alison, "and I'm awfully sorry. Mr. Strachan would love it the minute you're really in ... but till you are——"

"We're in right enough," George said bitterly, "in up to the neck. Mother says so. It's only the President hasn't said 'Go' yet—you know what Governments are, 'waiting and seeing,' and all that rot. Look at your own! And everybody getting killed all the time."

"I know," Alison said. "But that's what makes the difference. We *are* getting killed, all the time, even here in London."

George put the little flag in his pocket. "I came to wish you a happy New Year, Alison," he said with an effort to speak pleasantly. "I'll have to get you something else. There's some little silver things for the shop for you, Barbara, and a machine-gun for Jasper. Perhaps the partickler Mr. Strachan wouldn't mind having that on his roof to fire at the Huns when they come over."

"Won't you let me keep the flag?" Alison asked. "Then if ever America...."

"If ever," George interrupted scornfully. "That's all you know about it. If you'll wait you'll jolly well see this time. And you won't wait long!"

But he kept the flag in his pocket; and that night he put it in an envelope to keep it clean.

George was right. She didn't have to wait so very much longer, for on April 6th, America declared war on Germany, and he appeared directly after breakfast waving a Stars and Stripes large enough to have covered the doll's house like a tablecloth, so they hung it out of the nursery window instead, and Jasper "t'luted" it when he went out in his pram. And Alison got the little flag from George and put it between that of England and France on the doll's house, and he further presented the Strachans with two little khaki gunners to man the gun on the roof, for there were rumors to the effect that London would get it particularly hot that summer. The Huns were so angry about America.

That very morning great-uncle Jasper came to see the children, and gave each of them, including George, a bright new half-crown.

Jasper was much pleased with his, and refused to be parted from it even after Nannie had dressed him to go out. He declared he would hold it exceedingly tight and not "jop" it. Nannie had taken him with her down to the kitchen to get the list of wanted groceries from cook, and before you could say "knife" he had raced into the scullery, mounted a chair, and thrust the new half-crown down into one of the divisions of the knife-machine, proclaiming triumphantly that it was "a bid money-box." And there the half-crown remains to this day unless somebody has been demobilized who understands Kent's knife-machines.

Nannie hated to take Jasper to shops instead of the Park, but she had to do it sometimes because things had to be got and there was no one else to fetch them; besides, the "pram was handy for parcels." He thoroughly enjoyed these expeditions and certainly cheered up the shopping of other people.

That morning when they arrived at the grocer's there was the usual tired, cross-looking throng of housewives bearing string bags, irascible old gentlemen with leather ones, and the inevitable slate with the restrictive announcement: "No Matches. No Jam. No Bacon. No Tea. No Cheese. No Lard."

"Tut, tut," muttered Nannie. "No cheese again!"

"No tzeeze adain," Jasper instantly repeated, but in ringing tones that might have indicated glorious news, and everybody laughed.

"Bless his heart," said Nannie when she got home, "he does his bit as well as anybody."

Alison was always ready enough to take care of Jasper, and was thoroughly trustworthy as regards letting no harm befall him; but she looked upon such "minding" in the light of "war work," and her methods were somewhat austere.

She was annoyed that he should constantly interrupt mummy when she read aloud the latest war news from *The Times* by frivolous calls for admiration of his clock-work rabbit, and that mummy never failed to respond. And Alison was positively shocked that he could go on playing absorbedly with the said rabbit even when mummy read to them a letter from daddy in France.

She forgot that, for Jasper, daddy was chiefly known as a picture in a frame that stood on a table by mummy's bed, whereof he kissed the glass, making a smudge on it, every night when he had said his prayers; whereas the familiar rabbit was furry and comforting to carry, and went across the floor in a succession of exciting hops when it was wound up.

After all, Jasper was but a very little boy.

As for Barbara, she followed where Jasper led. Barbara was no sort of use for minding. Yet she could devise most delightful games, and gave dolls' tea-parties when all the vanished delicacies that used to grace such festivities before the war appeared again. So lavish was she with chocolate éclaires and cream buns and "white and pink sugar cakes" that Alison, the conscientious, was moved to expostulate, exclaiming: "What about the rationing, Barbara?"

"There's no war in fairyland," Barbara answered serenely, "and this is a fairy tea, so you can have as many lumps of sugar as ever you like."

Jasper was a cause of anxiety at these functions, because he *would* put a whole plate in his mouth at once. The V.A.D. doll fell over backward, she was so shocked. Such voluptuous gastronomic joys as chocolate éclaires and cream buns woke no responsive thrill in Jasper's breast, for he had never either seen nor tasted one or the other, so when called upon to pretend to eat something, he seized the nearest thing of handy size.

The children's house had a basement, but George's mother lived in a beautiful Willet house that had none, so that autumn he and his mother and their maids used to run over "to spend the raid" with Jasper's household when the first maroons sounded.

After the Zeppelin raids the doll's house had been brought down from the nursery to a room in the basement where there was a gas fire, and the children used to play with it and enact many thrilling dramas while the raids were going on. As George had prophesied, London got it particularly hot during the harvest moon of 1917, with five raids in eight nights.

They had all just got back from a holiday in the country and, with the exception of Barbara, who was gun-shy and hated the noise, they really felt the strain far less than the grown-ups.

Jasper usually slept most of the time in his mother's arms, but after a particularly loud crash would rouse himself to murmur with sleepy complacency: "That was a good one. We got 'em that time."

But Barbara, when the barrage was unusually deafening and prolonged, remarked rather piteously: "How it must 'asturb the poor angels!"

It was during the very last raid of all, in May of the following year, that something happened to the doll's house. It was on a Sunday night, and the maroons didn't start till eleven o'clock. George and his household hurried over as soon as he had got some clothes on, and Jasper woke up and was very talkative and cheerful. Arrayed in a blue dressing-gown and bed-shoes, he ran about the room, interfering with George and his sisters in their arrangement of the Strachan family, and shouting lustily in concert with the louder crashes.

He wasn't often allowed to touch the interior of the doll's house, for his methods were too Bolshevist, and he was inclined to instigate conduct wholly opposed to the characters of so *douce* and respectable a family.

That night Barbara insisted that Jeannie, the maid, and the baby should take refuge under one of the counters, while Mr. and Mrs. Strachan and the shop assistants crouched behind the other.

It happened that just then Jasper had developed a mania for collecting smooth, round stones, and Alison had suggested he should form an ammunition dump to supply the Strachans' machine-gun. This dump he was allowed to build near the stumpy little low oak table on casters that had supported the doll's house from the time it was first built. Mummy had carefully explained to him that he must on no account throw the stones *at* anything, because Jasper came of three generations of left-hand bowlers, and had already shown that he could throw a ball in the direction he wanted it to go. So far he had never thrown a stone either at things or people, for he was a kind little soul and no more disobedient than the generality of small boys of three. But he carried a stone in his hand all day long unless Nannie discovered it and took it from him. He liked the feel of it, its smoothness, its roundness, its vast potentialities.

That night he had been shooed away from the doll's house half a dozen times, for Alison and George were absorbed in a thrilling play in which the Strachans captured a German spy who was guiding enemy air-craft by means of forbidden lights.

Just as the "Archies" were barking their loudest, and an unmistakable bomb dropped somewhere, Jasper, on the other side of the room, gave a whoop and let fly the stone he had in his left hand straight at the doll's-house roof. It took one of the wooden chimneys broadside on and broke it clean off, narrowly missing the massed heads of his two sisters and George, which were luckily almost inside the house absorbed in the spy drama.

It also cracked some of the neat little slates on the roof.

There was a general consternation and excitement, and Jasper scurried across the room to secure another stone from the dump, when he would have undoubtedly had a shot at the other chimney had not Nannie caught him and held him tight.

Then it was that Alison astonished her family, for instead of demanding instant and condign punishment for her destructive little brother, she danced about the room and burst into poetry, shouting at the top of her voice:

The Strachans are in the War Zone, their house has been hit,

They've caught a bad spy and they're all done their bit.

"She's a most onaccountable child, Miss Alison," said Nannie to cook next day; "she was actually sorry that the stone didn't go right through the roof, an' you'd have thought she'd have gone on ever so ... anyway, it kept them from caring much about the raid."

CONCERNING CHRIS AND EASTER (1916)

Easter is the only girl, a sort of happy afterthought at the end of a long family of five boys, with six years between her and her next brother.

Chris is the only precious child, born after a good many years of marriage to devoted and adoring parents.

Easter doesn't think much of boys. They are common as blackberries in her family and she is keenly sensible of her own distinction in having, as she puts it, "chosen to come as a girl."

Thus it came about that her mental attitude struck Chris with something of a shock; not wholly unpleasant; stimulating; the tingle of resentment tempered by a thrill of amused surprise. It was so odd and new to meet anyone who felt like that.

Besides, till he came to live in Easter's village he had been rather lonely, and she supplied a felt want. Especially had this been so in the last two bewildering years, for his parents had seemed less absorbed in him than was quite dutiful. And for the last year his father had vanished altogether to that mysterious place that swallowed up so many pleasant and familiar folk; that overshadowing, omnipotent, vastly extending region known as "the front."

Easter, on her part, welcomed the society of Chris. She, too, was lonely by reason of the very same cause as Chris. Little girls were scarce in that village and Easter's mother was busy all day long with war work of one sort and another, and owing to the same cause Chris's governess, Miss Radley, only gave him her society during the bare hours of lessons, which lessons had for some time been shared by Easter.

Now Easter was much better at lessons than Chris; much quicker, in most things far more intelligent and receptive. Only in arithmetic did Chris shine, and in this subject he had soared away from Easter and did abstruse calculations in the end of the book all by himself with Miss Radley.

Easter was born on an Easter Day, and this year she was eight years old. Chris was born on Christmas Day, and last Christmas he was eight. Therefore, in spite of his prowess in arithmetic, he maintains that he is a year older than Easter.

"Weren't you born in 1908?" he demands sternly.

"Ye-es," answers Easter, "on an Easter Sunday. They *were* so pleased."

"And I," says Chris, "was born in 1907. Take seven from eight and what remains?"

"One, but it isn't a real, whole one," Easter objects.

No one knows this better than Chris, but he stoutly maintains: "A year's a year, and you're either born in it or you're not—so there."

However, in spite of this and many other differences of opinion, they had decided to get married when they came to what Easter's nurse calls "a suitable age."

As a rule Chris follows blindly where Easter leads, giving in to her stronger will and considerably stronger body, though not always without protest.

Easter is tall for her age and very muscular. She has a gentle, early-Victorian, regularly featured, delicately tinted face, with a high forehead, abundant curly, fair hair, and large pathetic blue eyes that are entirely misleading. In fact, her appearance is as unlike her real character as it is possible for such an extremely agreeable exterior to be. She looks all softness and gravity and gentle melancholy. Whereas she is a ruthless and determined young person who cares nothing for "moral suasion" and less for punishments and penalties, provided she gets her own way.

Chris, on the contrary, is soft-hearted and easily ruled through his affections. He would rather not be disobedient and troublesome unless such breakings of the law are expressly commanded by Easter.

But to be called a "muff" is more than he can bear, and rather than Easter should think this of him he will offend his whole dynasty of friends.

Chris and Easter were sitting under a hedge brilliant with scarlet hips and cloudy with "traveler's joy." The hedge topped a fairly steep bank, with a ditch full of muddy water at the bottom of the bank.

A heated argument was in progress as to the names of their eight daughters. Easter had already chosen the names, and they ran as follows: Irene, Semolina, Rosalind, Majorca, Minorca, Vinolia, Larola, and Salonica. Chris objected to Semolina and Vinolia.

"I hate semolina," he observed gloomily, "almost as bad as I hate rice."

"But it sounds so much nicer."

"And Vinolia, too—greasy stuff you smear on chapped legs."

"It's got a lovely smell," said Easter.

"And why," demanded Chris, who was in a bold and captious mood, "should there be eight of 'em? Why can't there be some boys?"

"I won't have boys, I tell you," Easter declared firmly. "Girls are far prettier."

"*Are* they?" asked Chris incredulously. "I've never seen any pretty ones."

Instead of asking "Where are your eyes?" Easter said huffily, in life-like imitation of nurse: "That's as it may be. Anyway they wear far prettier clothes."

"You don't," Chris pointed out.

Easter looked down at her extremely short and faded navy-blue skirt, at her long legs stuck out in front of her, at her muddy boots, at the large hole in the knee of her stocking. Save for the said skirt she was dressed almost exactly like Chris, in muffin cap, reefer and brass buttons.

"Sometimes I do," she maintained; "but anyway, Irene, Semolina, and Rosalind, and Majorca, and Minorca, and Vinolia, and Larola, and Salonica will all have lovely frocks, silk ninon, with sashes. Chris, they'll be perfectly sweet, and we'll make them walk two and two in front of us to church."

"I tell you," Chris declared, unmoved by this entrancing vision, "that I don't *want* so many daughters. I don't like them, I don't want 'em and I won't have 'em."

"Then," Easter ejaculated in breathless tones that should have warned him, "I shan't marry you."

"I don't care," the callous Chris announced. "The country wants men. I heard my daddy say so the last time he was home. There's far too many women as it is. They can't fight."

"Can't they?" the indignant Easter exclaimed ironically, and giving Chris a vigorous and wholly unexpected push, rolled him down the steep bank and into the ditch with a mighty splash; and then, adding insult to injury, she dug her heels into the wet grass, and taking off with skill and surety, jumped over his prostrate body on to the road, whereupon she ran away, laughing derisively.

Chris got most uncommonly wet, for the bottom of the ditch was slimy and soft. Even after he had struggled to his feet they slipped about and sank in far over the tops of his boots. And when he did manage to scramble up the bank to the road, he certainly looked a deplorable object, covered with mud and green slime and with water oozing from every bit of him. He stamped his feet and rubbed them on the wet grass that bordered the road without much visible betterment.

There was no going back through the village in such a plight, so he climbed the first five-barred gate he saw and started on a long cross-country journey that was to bring him home by unfrequented ways. He found the unfrequented ways, for he didn't meet a soul, but he lost his bearings altogether. The wind got up and there followed cold, gusty showers of rain and hail. He felt chilled and miserable and dreadfully tired. Field after field he traversed and yet found no familiar landmarks, till, having toiled uphill over a heavy ploughed field, he reached a road that stood fairly high, and below him on the far horizon he recognized the square tower of his own church. He plodded on and on till at last he trotted wearily up his own drive, and there he saw that not only Miss Radley but the three maids were all gathered on the steps of the front door. The moment Miss Radley saw him she ran toward him, exclaiming:

"Oh, Chris! Where *have* you been? We were getting so anxious. Do you know it's half-past five? My dear boy, how wet you are! Come in and get changed at once."

The maids went back into the house when they saw Chris, and Miss Radley hurried him in and upstairs, not even waiting to make him wipe his feet.

"We've been so anxious," she repeated. "I went to Easter's, and she said you'd parted ever so long ago. Why did you go off by yourself like that?"

Chris was half in, half out of his sailor blouse by this time, and mumbled something about having got tired of Easter.

Miss Radley didn't worry him much with questions, nor did she comment severely upon his dirty state. She was extraordinarily kind and got her hands all over mud in helping him to take off his boots; and it was not until he was lying luxuriously in a hot bath that it struck him as odd that his mother didn't come to him. All the time, too, he had the feeling that Miss Radley wanted to tell him something and yet she couldn't seem to begin.

"Where's mummy?" he asked at last. "Isn't she back yet? I wish she'd come and talk to me."

Miss Radley looked queerly at him, almost as though she were going to cry. "Chris dear," she said, and waited for quite a long time, "mummy has had to go away...."

"Away! For the night? Where to? Why?"

"Chris dear"—again Miss Radley seemed to find it difficult to go on—"she had a telegram, just after you went out, from the War Office, asking her to go at once. Your father is in a hospital at Boulogne, very ill ... wounded."

"Dangerously wounded?" asked Chris, who was familiar with war terms.

Miss Radley nodded, and two tears ran down her cheeks. "That's what it said."

"I think," said Chris, "I'd like to get out of this bath now."

When he was dressed he didn't seem to want the long-delayed tea, even though there was a beautiful brown egg and lovely buttered toast. In spite of the hot bath and a bright fire in the schoolroom he felt horrid, cold trickles running down his back all the time. He was extremely tired, too, yet only conscious of one overwhelming want—to be taken on his mother's knee and comforted. Miss Radley took him on hers and sat with him right in front of the fire. She was very kind and told him how sorry mummy had been to go off in such a hurry without saying good-bye, but there was just one train that would reach London that night if she caught it at the junction; and the squire, Easter's father, had driven her himself in his motor, and they just managed; and she was crossing to France that night in charge of a brother officer of dad's—she had her passport long ago.

Every now and then Miss Radley lightly touched his face, which was very hot, and then she would hold his hand, which was very cold. Half-asleep, Chris would murmur from time to time, "dangerously wounded," but somehow he couldn't feel about it as he knew he ought to feel. Though he adored his daddy, all he felt was this overpowering ache of longing for his mother.

Easter's scornful refusal to have any boys in her family had hurt him very much. He felt lonely and pushed out, somehow; and he badly wanted the one person who never failed in her appreciation of little boys, even if they were thin and small and not particularly good looking, and could not run so fast as ... certain little girls. He was conscious of being all these undesirable things, and yet he was convinced it was a great and glorious thing to be a boy, even if Easter didn't think so. Once, after a long and acrimonious discussion with her on this very subject, he had said to his mother: "I choosed to come as a boy, didn't I?"

"God chose," said his mother gravely.

"Me and God settled it together," Chris announced complacently, and his mother got up suddenly and looked in a cupboard for something she never found.

In Chris's mind God and Father Christmas were inextricably mixed up. He had no fear of either one or the other. Both were beneficent and considerate and ready to give people their choice both as to presents or other things.

Yet when he was put to bed that night he couldn't dream of pleasant, soothing things, but was pursued by eight strong daughters in embroidered ninon frocks and pink sashes, who formed themselves into a solid phalanx and drove him to the edge of an awful precipice, and were just pushing him over ... when he would wake to find Miss Radley standing beside his bed, looking anxious and troubled, shading a candle with her hand.

The war had not touched Easter very nearly. Her mother had forbidden nurse to talk about it to her; and her father (judging her sensitiveness wholly from her gentle, Early-Victorian appearance) was careful to keep all frightening or depressing news from her as far as was possible. All her life she had been sheltered and adored and spared and spoiled. Her brothers, being so much older, had "given in" to her from the very first, and although the two eldest were fighting—one in the navy, the other in the army—their doings did not seem to affect her particularly. And of the three still at school she had, of late, seen very little, for in the holidays they were always doing O.T.C. training, or making munitions somewhere.

Yet one thing had impressed her during the last two years. She was always hearing that some of their acquaintances had "lost" a son, a brother, or a husband. They did not talk of "killed" or "missing" to Easter; but they did speak of this continual and mysterious "loss," and with the queer secretive puzzledom of childhood she never asked people outright what they meant by the phrase.

It worried her, this continual losing. She never heard that these lost ones got found again. Suppose she herself got lost in this irretrievable way? How dreadful it would be. What would her family do? In justice to Easter one must allow that the thought of her people's consternation quite overshadowed any possibly unpleasant consequences to herself.

She had never discussed the question with Chris, who knew a lot about the war and wanted to talk about it to the exclusion of more interesting topics— such as daughters. But this was easily overruled. Moreover, Easter's mother had decided that far too much was said about the war in Chris's hearing, and she had asked Miss Radley to warn him not to talk about it to Easter lest it should upset her.

Miss Radley had her own opinion of Easter's sensibility. She had not taught the children for six months without discovering which was the more susceptible and imaginative. But she did as she was bid, and Chris had done his best to obey in his turn. Perhaps in a lofty masculine way he was rather proud that he should be allowed to know things closely hidden from the domineering Easter, and was therefore the less anxious to share his knowledge with her.

He whole-heartedly admired Easter. She was so strong, so good at things, so invariably cheerful and well, with a never-failing fund of good spirits and energy. It is very possible that one of her chief attractions for him lay in the fact that she seemed so entirely outside those great and grave anxieties that obsessed everybody else.

Easter was brought up to understand that any "career" that she chose was open to her. She should have an equal chance with any of her brothers; she might be a doctor for a factory inspector, or a police-woman, or go in for any art or craft she fancied. Literature, art, music, even the stage, were to be open to her, should she so wish. But, so far, her sole ambition was centred in the possession of a husband, a meek husband, and eight meek daughters to move and have their being at her decree.

It was the swing of the pendulum with a vengeance.

No one told Easter about Chris's daddy that afternoon. In the evening she prepared her lessons with her customary energy and intelligence, and giggled cheerfully from time to time at the recollection of Chris's comical appearance as he lay floundering in the ditch.

"That'll teach him," said Easter to herself, "whether it's to be daughters or not!"

Next morning at breakfast her mother said: "Miss Radley can't take you to-day, Easter dear, so it's no use your going over. They had very bad news yesterday, and Mrs. Denver has had to go to France. The major is very ill."

"Has Chris gone?" Easter asked.

"No, dear; but Miss Radley sent over a note quite early to say he has got a bad, feverish cold (he got so wet yesterday—it's a pity he didn't come back with you), and we don't know what it may turn to. So you must just take a holiday, for I'm due at the hospital supplies at ten, and shall be away all day."

"What's the matter with Major Denver?"

"I fear," said her mother, anxiously watching the earnest, delicately tinted face upturned to hers, "I fear he is very badly wounded."

"Oh!" said Easter, and she looked very grave.

"Be as happy as you can, my precious," her mother called to her as she drove away. "I'll get home as early as possible."

That was a very long day for Easter.

For one thing, it rained all the morning; for another, her father had to go a long way off on business connected with special constables, and couldn't take her; and Amelia, the usually cheerful housemaid, went about the house with red eyes and a perpetual sniff, because she had heard that morning she'd lost a cousin in the "big push on the Somme."

Amelia was distinctly depressing.

Easter knitted a few rows of her scarf—the scarf that was always begun by her and finished by somebody else because she got tired of it. She found she was missing Chris far more poignantly than was at all pleasant.

After all, even if he didn't always quite give in to her, he was good company; and Easter found herself remembering many kind things he had done. The chocolates he had always shared so generously, the apples so unequally divided always in her favor. Once when she fell off a wall and scratched her hands and tore her frock so badly, he hadn't laughed, and he was so seldom rough in play, only when unbearably provoked. Easter was too honest not to admit that even at the time.

It cleared up in the afternoon and she ran over to the Denvers' house to see if Chris was up yet and could play.

Emma, the parlormaid, was firm in her refusal to admit Easter.

"Master Chris is that bad, so feverish it might turn to anything, the doctor says. Miss Radley said no one was to come in, and she haven't left Master Chris a single minute herself. It's dreadful, and us all in such trouble about the major, too."

"You haven't lost him, have you?" Easter asked.

"Good gracious! no, not yet, so far as we knows. But he's as bad as bad, and," she added, "if anything was to happen to Master Chris and his ma away an' all—but, there! I can't bear to think of it. You run along home, Miss Easter. I'll tell Miss Radley you came to ask."

And the door was shut in Easter's face.

Next day the news was no better. Even Easter's mother could not keep from her the universal anxiety as to Major Denver. He had been their doctor for a year before the war, and in that time had managed to endear himself to everybody.

It was said he had taken a country practice because he thought the bracing air would be good for Chris. Every soul in the village felt a special right to know the latest news of the major, and Miss Radley had the telegrams pinned on the front door as soon as she got them.

All day long people came up the drive to read these telegrams, and presently there was a bit of white paper as well, concerning Chris, for the doctor's little son lay grievously sick at home, while his father, they feared, was dying of his wounds in France. A white-capped hospital nurse had come to help Miss Radley.

Easter was a very lonely little girl. She felt, too, that in some inexplicable fashion she was shut out from things, that more was happening than she was allowed to know; and, worst of all, Chris had so entirely disappeared that she began to fear that he, too, was lost, and they were afraid to tell her.

At the end of nearly a week she felt she could not bear this furtiveness and suspense a minute longer, and she determined to go to Chris's house and find out for herself just what had happened and was happening. She would not ring the bell. She would go round to the side of the house and see if the schoolroom window was open, and get in and find Miss Radley and force her to tell the truth. If Chris was lost, then she, Easter, must herself set forth to find him without more delay.

All fell out as she had planned.

The schoolroom window, which opened like a door divided down the middle, was open, and Miss Radley, with her back to it, sat at the table, writing.

Easter could move quietly as a cat when it suited her. She came in without making a sound, and stood just behind Miss Radley, who was so absorbed she noticed nothing.

"Have you lost Chris, Miss Radley?" Easter asked loudly.

Miss Radley started violently, and Easter came round to her side, and she noticed that Miss Radley's usually round, rosy face was pale and much less round than it used to be.

"Oh, Easter dear, how you startled me! Don't suggest such a dreadful thing! We're awfully anxious, with his mother away and all this other trouble, but ... we must hope always, always hope—for if anything happened to Chris...."

"What *has* happened to Chris?" Easter asked, searching the very soul of Miss Radley with her large clear gaze.

"He got so wet after he left you that day last week—I can't think how—and he got a real bad chill, and now there are all sorts of complications—and his temperature keeps up so."

"What are complications?" Easter interrupted.

"You wouldn't understand.... Oh, Easter, child, don't stare at me like that! Aren't you sorry?"

"I know how Chris got so wet," Easter said slowly. "I pushed him into the ditch."

Miss Radley drew back a little from Easter; then she put out her hand and laid it on the child's arm.

"I expect it was only in fun ... you couldn't know...."

"Can't I play with him a bit? Is it catching?" Easter's voice was still quite loud and matter-of-fact. "It's rather dull and lonely for me."

"For *you!*" Miss Radley echoed indignantly. "Don't you understand? Don't you care, you hard child? But you never did care for anybody but yourself."

"Does Chris?"

"Yes, indeed he does. He's always been a dear, kind boy. Easter, you must go home. I can't stop to talk to you now. Try to think about other people a little...."

Miss Radley did not finish her sentence, for Easter had gone from her as silently as she had come. For a minute the governess sat quite still. Then she sighed and shivered, and went on with her letter.

Easter fled down the Denvers' drive and out into the road, but she didn't go home. She ran and ran till she could run no more, and dropping into a walk, turned downhill along a winding lane thickly bordered by trees so high that they almost met overhead, forming an arch. The light in this avenue was curiously lurid, for the trees were beeches, and though rapidly thinning, were still gorgeous in reds and yellows. The avenue led to a church in the next parish (Easter had run such a long way), and she had been there quite lately with Chris to a fruit and flower service in aid of the local hospital. Miss Radley had taken them both, and now Easter remembered there were very large vegetable marrows at the base of one of the pillars, and wondered if they were still there. She and Chris had sat next each other at that service, and during the sermon he had let her hold his knife. It had a corkscrew and a thing for taking stones out of horses' hoofs, as well as blades, and all were very difficult to open. Chris was good about lending his things. And he never told of people. What did old Raddles mean when she called her hard? She did care for Chris, but she wasn't going to say so to Raddles. Yet Raddles looked awfully sad. Supposing they *had* lost Chris, after all, and were afraid to say? Supposing she, Easter, got lost, now, to-day? This was a long, lonely, unfamiliar road, with such a queer light in it. Supposing it were enchanted and she couldn't find her way back? Then she would be like all those sons she had heard about lately. Her heart began to beat very fast. Ah! somebody was coming up the road. She would ask her way. It would be dreadful to be lost.

A very tall lady came toward her walking slowly up the hill. She was dressed in black, with a long thin veil turned back from her face. She looked restlessly from side to side, as though trying to find somebody in the shadows. This seemed quite natural to Easter. Timidity or shyness with strangers was unknown to her. She was glad to see somebody, and the tall lady's face was very gentle.

"Have *you* lost anybody?" Easter asked as they met.

The tall lady stopped, and though she looked straight down at Easter, the child was uncomfortably conscious that she didn't really see her.

"I have lost my only son," said the lady.

"You, too!" cried Easter, and what she could not say to Miss Radley she found it easy to say now to this pale lady who looked at her so strangely. "Oh, I *am* sorry!"

And she took one of the lady's hands in both her own.

The lady did not draw her hand away; with her eyes still fixed on Easter's face with that queer, unseeing look, she said: "Dear child! And you?"

"Not yet," said Easter. "Not yet—at least, they say so, but I'm dreadfully afraid."

"Don't be afraid," said the lady. "Don't be afraid. That's what he always said."

"Everyone," said Easter, and her hard little voice grew soft, "everyone seems losing sons and people. Won't you never, never find him again?"

Into that lady's face there leapt a sudden radiance as when a clearly burning lamp is carried into a dark room. Her eyes were luminous and bright, and Easter felt that she was really seeing her at last.

"We shall all find them again," she said almost joyously. "Everyone of us."

"Are you sure?" Easter questioned.

"In sure and certain hope," said the lady.

"In sure and certain hope," Easter repeated. "I like that. You *are* sure?"

"Absolutely. Tell me, dear, who is it you are anxious about?"

Hand in hand they had started slowly to mount the hill.

"It's Chris," she said. "He plays with me a lot and we do lessons together ... and they won't let me see him, and I want to tell him I'm sorry."

"But why won't they let you see him?"

"Because they're afraid they'll lose him—I heard *that*, though Raddles denied it when I asked her."

"Then he's ill?"

"I suppose so."

The lady looked curiously at Easter. There was no doubt whatever that she was troubled, and yet ... how oddly the child spoke.

As they walked on, hand in hand, the lady said, more to herself than to Easter: "Does the road wind uphill all the way?"

"No," said Easter; "when we get to the end of this it's quite flat."

When they came to the main road Easter took her hand out of the lady's. "I know my way now," she said. "Good-bye."

The lady stooped and kissed her. "I should write to Chris if I were you," she said. "He'll probably like a letter very much when he's a little better."

Easter nodded and started to run, with that swift, long-distance, steady running that had so often worn out Chris; that was his admiration and his despair. And as she ran she repeated over and over again: "In sure and certain hope" all the way.

She would write to Chris directly she got in. Her copies were always neater than his.

But she couldn't do it the minute she got in, for tea was ready, and her mother there to have it with her. Her mother looked pleased, too. Better news had come from France. There was hope that Major Denver might pull through, after all; and she had seen Miss Radley, and Chris's temperature was nearly down to normal.

It was a lovely tea; and directly after it Easter sat down at her mother's desk and wrote to Chris. Very large, with beautiful up-and-down strokes:

"DEAR CHRIS,

"I'm sory I pushed you. Sum of them shall be boys. The ones with the names you don't like. Please don't get lost.

"Your loving
"EASTER."

She licked the flap of the envelope with copious completeness, and in one corner of the address, very thick and black, in inch-long printed letters was the word "EARGUNT."

Milton Keynes UK
Ingram Content Group UK Ltd.
UKHW030740071024
449371UK00006B/682

9 789362 098054